VIBE CODING FO

Turn Your Ideas into Apps Without Writing Code - A Practical
Guide to Building with AI

AKASH KUMAR NAYAK

Disclaimer: This book is for informational purposes only. The rapidly evolving field of AI and "Vibe Coding" means information may not always be current or perfectly accurate. The author and publisher assume no liability for errors or omissions. The techniques described are provided without warranty; use AI tools and generated code at your own risk, understanding potential bugs and security issues. Always test thoroughly and exercise caution, especially with sensitive data. This book does not constitute professional technical, legal, or security advice.

Akash Kumar Nayak

ISBN: 9798280615250

INTRODUCTION

Do you have ideas? Brilliant ones? Ideas for apps, websites, tools, or digital experiences that could solve a problem, delight users, or simply bring your unique creative vision into the world? Perhaps it's a simple website to showcase your art, a handy tool to organize your research, or even the seed of a business concept. You can see it clearly in your mind's eye.

But then comes the familiar roadblock: "I don't know how to code."

For too long, the incredible power of software creation has felt locked away, accessible only to those with specialized technical skills or significant financial resources. How many potentially amazing projects have withered in the "Idea Graveyard" simply because the path from concept to reality seemed too steep, too complex, too *coded*?

If you're an artist, a writer, an entrepreneur, a maker, an educator, or simply someone brimming with ideas but lacking a traditional programming background, this frustration is likely all too familiar. You have the vision, the creativity, the understanding of what needs to exist – but the tools seemed out of reach.

Until now.

Something revolutionary is happening at the intersection of human creativity and Artificial Intelligence. Powerful AI assistants have emerged, capable not just of understanding our language, but of translating our descriptions, our conversations, our *vibes*, into functional software code. This is the dawn of **Vibe Coding**.

Imagine describing your app idea as you would to a helpful collaborator, focusing on what it should do and how it should feel. Imagine that collaborator instantly generating the underlying code, building a working prototype right before your eyes. Imagine guiding the process through iteration and intuition, refining the design and functionality through simple conversation, without getting bogged down in complex syntax or obscure algorithms.

This isn't science fiction anymore. Vibe Coding is making digital creation accessible in ways previously unimaginable. It's shifting the focus from the intricate mechanics of writing code to the inherently human skills of **vision, communication, creativity, and critical thinking.**

This book is your guide to embracing this revolution.

"Vibe Coding for Creators" is written specifically for *you* – the non-technical visionary, the creative mind ready to build. Forget dense programming manuals and intimidating jargon. Our journey together will be practical, accessible, and empowering. We will:

- **Demystify Vibe Coding:** Understand what it is, where it came from, and how it fundamentally changes the creation process.
- **Meet Your AI Co-Creators:** Discover the user-friendly tools and platforms that make Vibe Coding possible today.
- **Master the Art of the Prompt:** Learn how to communicate effectively with AI to get the results you want.
- **Build Your First Project:** Walk step-by-step through creating a simple application using Vibe Coding – focusing entirely on the process, not the code itself.
- **Explore the Possibilities:** See the kinds of cool projects well-suited for this approach.
- **Vibe Responsibly:** Understand the potential pitfalls and learn practical tips for staying safe and smart.
- **Look to the Future:** Glimpse where this exciting technology might be heading.

This is not about turning you into a traditional programmer overnight. It's about unlocking the creator already inside you, giving you a powerful new medium to express your ideas and solve problems. It's about bridging the gap between your imagination and tangible digital reality.

The future of creation is becoming more conversational, more intuitive, more accessible. Your ideas are valuable, your perspective is needed, and the tools are finally here to help you bring them to life.

Are you ready to find your vibe? Let's start creating.

<u>PREFACE</u>

For years, I've been fascinated by the intersection of creativity and technology. I've spoken with countless artists, entrepreneurs, educators, and makers – people brimming with brilliant, innovative ideas for how digital tools could enhance their work, connect their communities, or simply bring more joy into the world. And yet, time and again, I heard the same lament: "I'd love to build that, but I just don't know how to code."

It felt like witnessing a vast, untapped reservoir of human ingenuity held back by a dam of technical complexity. The digital world, arguably the most powerful creative medium ever invented, seemed accessible only to a select group who had mastered its intricate languages. This "digital divide" wasn't just about access to devices; it was about access to the fundamental tools of creation.

Then, almost overnight, things began to change. The rapid advancements in Artificial Intelligence, particularly Large Language Models, started producing results that felt like science fiction just a short time ago. Suddenly, AI could understand natural language with remarkable nuance, and crucially, it could translate human intent into functional computer code. I watched, fascinated, as people began experimenting – describing ideas in plain English and seeing AI assistants sketch out the digital blueprints.

The emergence of what the tech community playfully dubbed "Vibe Coding" felt like more than just a new tool; it felt like the first crack in that dam. Here was a pathway, however new and imperfect, for non-technical creators to bypass the traditional barriers and directly participate in building their own software. It wasn't about replacing programmers; it was about *expanding* the definition of who gets to be a creator in the digital age.

That's why I felt compelled to write this book. While the potential of Vibe Coding is immense, the landscape can also be confusing. There's hype, there are valid concerns about risks, and much of the discussion can quickly veer into technical jargon inaccessible to the very people who stand to benefit most.

My goal with "Vibe Coding for Creators" is simple: to provide a clear, practical, and honest guide specifically for the non-technical visionary. This book is for the artist who wants a portfolio, the baker who needs an order form, the writer dreaming of an interactive story, the activist building a community tool – for anyone who has felt that spark of a digital idea but thought coding was beyond their reach.

We'll cut through the noise, focusing on what you actually need to know to get started. We'll explore the tools accessibly, practice the art of prompting, walk through building a real project without getting lost in code, and importantly, discuss how to approach this new power responsibly and safely.

This is not a traditional programming book. It's an invitation. An invitation to experiment, to create, and to finally bridge the gap between your imagination and digital reality. The tools are evolving rapidly, and the journey is just beginning, but the opportunity for empowerment is here now.

I truly believe that the most exciting innovations often come from those who bring fresh perspectives and deep domain knowledge from outside the traditional tech world. My hope is that this book serves as a catalyst, empowering you to bring your unique voice and valuable ideas into the digital landscape.

The future is vibey. Let's build it together.

(Author's Name – Akash Kumar Nayak)

Table of Contents

A.K.Nayak

CHAPTER 1: UNLOCK YOUR INNER CODER: WELCOME TO VIBE CODING

This Chapter Covers

- **Problem:** Lack of coding skills prevents great digital ideas ("Idea Graveyard").
- **Traditional Barriers:** Learning code (hard/slow), hiring devs (costly), no-code (limited).
- **Solution: Vibe Coding:** Use AI (LLMs) to generate code from natural language & feedback. Focus on feel/outcome, guide AI intuitively.
- **Skill Shift:** From writing code to articulating vision & guiding AI.
- **Example:** Designer built a tool via AI conversation, bypassing barriers.
- **Book Purpose:** Guide non-programmers on practical, responsible Vibe Coding.
- **Key Message:** Vibe Coding empowers non-coders; requires practice & responsibility.

"The best way to predict the future is to invent it."

- Alan Kay

Have you ever felt it? That spark? That brilliant flash of an idea for an app, a website, a tool – something digital that could solve a problem, connect people, organize your life, or just bring a little bit of joy or beauty into the world? Maybe it arrived in the shower, during a walk, or in that hazy space just before sleep. It felt vivid, *real*. You could almost see it, touch it, imagine people using it, benefiting from it, loving it.

Perhaps it was an idea for a simple website to showcase your art, finally giving your paintings or photographs the beautiful online gallery they deserve. Maybe it was a tool to help you manage recipes, letting you easily find that perfect dish you cooked months ago. Or perhaps something more ambitious – a platform to connect local volunteers with opportunities in your community, a unique game concept unlike anything you've seen, or a clever little app to help you track your habits and finally stick to those New Year's resolutions.

The idea shines brightly in your mind's eye. It feels important. It feels *possible*.

And then… the crash. The familiar, sinking feeling as the practicalities set in.

"But I don't know how to code."

How many incredible ideas have stalled right there, at that exact point? How many potentially world-changing, life-improving, or simply delightful digital creations currently reside only in the realm of imagination, locked away behind the seemingly impenetrable wall of technical expertise? We could call it the "Idea Graveyard," a vast, unseen landscape populated by the ghosts of brilliant concepts that never saw the light of day simply because their creators didn't possess the specific, complex skills of software development.

You're not alone in this frustration. Far from it. You might be an artist whose medium is paint or clay, not Python or JavaScript. You might be a writer whose craft lies in weaving words, not algorithms. You could be a small business owner, a passionate baker whose expertise is in sourdough, not software architecture. You might be a teacher, a community organizer, a therapist, a student – someone with deep knowledge in your own field, brimming with ideas born from your unique experience, but feeling utterly excluded from the process of building the digital tools that increasingly shape our world.

The traditional path to bringing a digital idea to life often feels like a daunting, multi-pronged obstacle course.

First, there's the **"Learn to Code"** route. This involves dedicating hundreds, if not thousands, of hours to learning complex programming languages, understanding arcane syntax, grappling with abstract concepts like data structures and algorithms, and mastering intricate development environments. It's like deciding you want to build a bookshelf and being told you first need to become a master carpenter, fell your own trees, mill the lumber, and forge your own tools. While immensely rewarding for those who pursue it, it's a massive commitment, often impractical for someone whose primary passion and expertise lie elsewhere. The learning curve is steep, progress can feel slow, and the initial excitement for your idea can easily dwindle under the weight of technical frustration.

Then there's the **"Hire a Developer"** option. This seems more direct, but it comes with its own set of challenges. Finding the right developer or agency can be difficult. Communicating your vision accurately, especially without a shared technical language, can lead to misunderstandings and costly revisions. And, perhaps most significantly, professional software development is expensive. Getting even a relatively simple application built can cost thousands, or tens of thousands, of dollars – often placing it far out of reach for individuals, startups, or non-profits operating on tight budgets. Your brilliant idea remains grounded, not by technical inability this time, but by financial constraints.

Finally, there are **"No-Code/Low-Code"** platforms. These tools have emerged as a fantastic step forward, allowing users to build applications using visual interfaces, dragging and dropping pre-built components. They have genuinely democratized certain types of software creation and are invaluable for many tasks. However, they often come with limitations. You might find yourself constrained by the platform's specific features, unable to implement that unique interaction or custom logic that makes your idea special. You're working with pre-fabricated building blocks, which is great for standard structures, but can sometimes feel restrictive if your vision doesn't quite fit the available molds.

So, the ideas pile up in the graveyard. The frustration mounts. It can feel like the digital world, this incredibly powerful realm of creation and connection, is largely off-limits unless you possess the keys of code or significant capital. The value locked away in those unbuilt ideas – the potential for personal fulfillment, community impact, business innovation, creative expression – remains unrealized.

But what if there was another way?

What if you could bypass the steepest parts of the coding learning curve? What if you could translate your vision into reality without needing a massive budget? What if you could create something truly custom, something uniquely *yours*, using the most natural interface you already possess – your own language?

Imagine sitting down, not with a complex code editor, but with something more like a conversational partner. Imagine describing your app idea, explaining the features you envision, outlining the user experience you desire, much like you'd explain it to a friend or colleague. And imagine this partner listening, understanding, and then... *building it*. Generating the underlying code, assembling the digital structure, bringing your concept to life, right before your eyes.

Imagine being able to say, "Okay, now make that button blue," or "Add a section here where users can upload photos," or "When someone clicks this, show them a thank you message," and seeing it happen. Imagine being able to guide the creation process through dialogue, through intuition, focusing on the *what* and the *why* – the core of your idea – rather than getting bogged down in the intricate *how* of traditional programming.

This isn't science fiction. This isn't a far-off dream. This is the emerging reality of **Vibe Coding**.

Welcome to a revolution in creation. Welcome to the possibility of unlocking your inner coder, not by forcing you to become a traditional programmer, but by providing you with tools that understand *you*.

What is Vibe Coding, Anyway?

The term "Vibe Coding" has recently emerged, bubbling up from the vibrant discussions within the tech community, particularly around the explosive advancements in Artificial Intelligence (AI). It might sound a bit whimsical, perhaps even vague, but it captures something profound about this new way of building software.

> At its heart, **Vibe Coding is the practice of using Artificial Intelligence, especially sophisticated Large Language Models (LLMs) like the ones powering tools like ChatGPT, to generate software code based on natural language descriptions and iterative feedback**.

Let's break that down:

- **Using Artificial Intelligence (AI):** This isn't about you writing code. It's about leveraging incredibly powerful AI systems that have been trained on vast amounts of text and code. These AI models have learned the patterns, syntax, and logic of various programming languages to an astonishing degree.
- **Large Language Models (LLMs):** Think of these as the "brains" behind the operation. They are complex algorithms designed to understand and generate human-like text. Crucially, their abilities extend beyond just writing essays or answering questions; they can also understand instructions about software and generate the corresponding code.
- **Generating Software Code:** The AI doesn't just give you advice; it actually writes the lines of code (in languages like HTML, CSS, JavaScript, Python, etc.) that form the building blocks of websites, apps, and other digital tools.
- **Natural Language Descriptions:** This is your primary input. Instead of writing function calculateTotal(price, quantity) { return price * quantity; }, you might simply say, "Create a function that takes a price and a quantity and returns the total cost." You interact using English (or other human languages), describing your intent.
- **Iterative Feedback:** It's rarely a one-shot process. You describe something, the AI builds it, you look at it, test it, and then provide

feedback. "That's close, but can you make the text larger?" "It's not saving the data correctly; can you fix that?" It's a conversation, a back-and-forth refinement process.

So, where does the "vibe" part come in? It refers to the *feeling* or *intuition-driven* nature of this process. Instead of meticulously planning every single logical step and translating it into precise code (the traditional approach), Vibe Coding often involves:

- **Focusing on the desired outcome and feel:** You guide the AI based on the overall experience you want to create. Does the app *feel* intuitive? Is the website *visually appealing*? Does the tool *behave* the way you envisioned?
- **Coding by "feel" or intuition:** You might make adjustments based on what seems right or looks good, rather than adhering strictly to pre-defined technical specifications. It allows for more organic, exploratory development, especially in the early stages.
- **Trusting the process (and the AI, with caution):** There's an element of letting go of granular control. You trust the AI to handle the complex coding details while you steer the ship at a higher level. This doesn't mean blind trust (we'll talk a *lot* more about responsible vibing later), but it involves accepting that you might not understand every single line of code the AI generates, as long as the result functions correctly and aligns with your vision.

Think of it like this:

- **Traditional Coding:** You are the master craftsperson, meticulously carving every detail of a wooden sculpture by hand, understanding the grain, the tools, the structure intimately. It requires deep skill and patience.
- **No-Code Platforms:** You are assembling a sculpture from a kit of high-quality, pre-made parts. It's faster and requires less specific skill, but you're limited to the parts provided in the kit.
- **Vibe Coding:** You are the sculptor describing your vision to an incredibly skilled, fast, and slightly unpredictable apprentice (the AI). You say, "I want a figure here, reaching upwards, with a sense of hope." The apprentice instantly carves it. You then refine: "Make the arm a bit higher," "Soften the expression," "Add more texture here." You guide the form based on your artistic intent and feeling, relying on the apprentice to execute the technical carving. You might not know *exactly* how the apprentice achieved that perfect curve, but you know it matches your vibe.

This approach represents a fundamental shift. It moves the primary skill from *writing code* to *articulating vision, providing clear instructions, evaluating results, and guiding an AI collaborator*. These are skills many creatives, makers, and entrepreneurs already possess in abundance. Vibe Coding essentially provides a bridge, allowing those skills to be applied directly to the creation of software.

A Spark of Possibility: Sarah's Story

Let me tell you about Sarah (a hypothetical, but representative, example). Sarah is a talented graphic designer who runs a small freelance business creating logos and branding for local businesses. She has a fantastic eye for aesthetics and a deep understanding of how visual identity can impact a company's success. For years, she'd dreamed of creating a simple online tool for her clients – something interactive where they could experiment with different color palettes and font combinations for their brand *before* committing to a final design direction.

She knew exactly how it should work: upload a logo, click on color swatches to see them applied instantly, select from a curated list of fonts to preview headlines and body text. It wasn't a massively complex idea, but it was beyond her technical capabilities. She looked into learning web development, but quickly felt overwhelmed by the sheer volume of information. She got quotes from web developers, but the cost was prohibitive for her small business budget. Her brilliant idea, a tool she knew her clients would love and that would streamline her own workflow, sat gathering dust in her mental "Idea Graveyard."

Then, Sarah started hearing about new AI tools that could help with coding. Initially skeptical ("Isn't that just for programmers?"), she decided to try one out – a popular chatbot known for its coding abilities. She started simply, tentatively.

"Can you create a basic webpage with a heading that says 'Brand Style Explorer'?"

To her amazement, the AI instantly generated a block of HTML code. She copied it into a simple online code playground and saw the heading appear. It felt like magic.

Emboldened, she continued the conversation. "Okay, now add a section below the heading where a user can upload an image file, like a logo." Again, the AI provided code. She tested it. It worked.

Over the next few evenings, Sarah continued this dialogue. She asked the AI to add color swatches. "When I click a color swatch, can you change the background color of the page to match?" She asked for a font selection dropdown. "Show some sample text that updates when I choose a different font." She described the layout she wanted, the spacing, the overall "clean and modern" vibe.

There were hiccups, of course. Sometimes the AI misunderstood her instructions. Sometimes the code it generated had bugs. But Sarah learned to refine her prompts, to describe the problems she encountered ("The font isn't changing when I select 'Roboto'") and ask the AI to fix them. She wasn't writing code, but she was *directing* the creation process, using her designer's eye to evaluate the results and her communication skills to guide the AI. She was, in essence, Vibe Coding.

Within a week, Sarah had a working prototype of her Brand Style Explorer. It wasn't perfect, but it was *real*. It was her idea, brought to life through conversation and iteration. The feeling of empowerment was immense. She had bypassed the traditional barriers and created something functional and valuable, something that would genuinely help her business and her clients. She hadn't needed to become a master coder; she had simply needed to articulate her vision and partner with the right tool.

Sarah's story isn't unique. All around the world, people just like you – artists, writers, educators, entrepreneurs, hobbyists – are beginning to discover the power of Vibe Coding. They are building websites, automating tasks, creating simple games, developing custom tools, and bringing long-dormant ideas out of the graveyard and into the digital world. They are experiencing the thrill of creation in a domain that previously felt inaccessible.

This Book: Your Guide to the Vibe

That thrill, that sense of empowerment, that ability to turn your unique ideas into tangible digital reality – that's what this book is all about. "Vibe Coding for Creators" is designed to be your friendly, accessible guide to navigating this exciting new landscape.

We won't be diving deep into complex programming theory or asking you to memorize obscure syntax. Instead, we'll focus on the practicalities, the mindset, and the creative possibilities of Vibe Coding, specifically for people who don't identify as traditional programmers.

Our journey together will cover:
- **Understanding the Core Concepts:** We'll delve a little deeper into what Vibe Coding is (and isn't), exploring its origins and the philosophy behind it in easy-to-understand terms (Chapters 2 & 3).
- **Meeting Your AI Co-Creators:** We'll introduce you to the key AI tools and platforms you can use to start vibe coding today, focusing on those that are most accessible for beginners (Chapter 4).
- **Your First Vibe Coding Project:** We'll walk you step-by-step through building a simple, practical application using the vibe coding process, focusing entirely on the conversational interaction and

iterative refinement – no actual code required for you to write!
(Chapter 5).

- **Mastering the Art of the Prompt:** You'll learn how to communicate effectively with your AI assistant, crafting clear instructions, providing useful context, and guiding it towards your desired outcome (Chapter 6).
- **Exploring the Possibilities (and Limitations):** We'll showcase the kinds of exciting projects you can realistically tackle with vibe coding and also discuss where its current limitations lie, helping you choose the right projects (Chapter 7).
- **Responsible Vibing: Staying Safe and Smart:** This is crucial. We'll address the potential pitfalls – bugs, security considerations, the risks of using code you don't fully understand – and provide practical, non-technical tips for testing your creations and using these powerful tools mindfully and safely (Chapter 8).
- **Looking Ahead: The Future is Vibey:** We'll explore where this technology might be heading and what it means for the future of creativity and software development (Chapter 9).
- **Getting Started: Finding Your Vibe:** We'll wrap up with encouragement and actionable next steps to help you embark on your own vibe coding adventures (Chapter 10).

Throughout this journey, our focus will remain firmly on **empowerment**. The goal is not just to teach you about Vibe Coding, but to equip you with the understanding, confidence, and practical skills to actually *use* it to bring *your* ideas to life.

We'll acknowledge the hype surrounding AI, but we'll also ground our discussion in reality. Vibe Coding isn't a magic wand that instantly creates flawless, complex software with zero effort. It's a powerful *tool* and a new *process* that requires learning, practice, critical thinking, and a degree of patience. It involves collaboration – a dance between your vision and the AI's capabilities.

And importantly, we'll emphasize the need for **mindful creation**. As Uncle Ben famously told Spider-Man, "With great power comes great responsibility." These AI tools offer incredible power to create, but using them effectively and safely requires awareness. We need to test what we build, think about the potential impact on users, and understand that the AI is an assistant, not an infallible oracle. This book will guide you not just in *how* to vibe code, but how to do so *responsibly*.

The wall between having a great digital idea and bringing it to life is crumbling. The keys to digital creation are no longer solely in the hands of those who speak the complex languages of code. Thanks to the rise of powerful AI and the emergence of Vibe Coding, the ability to build, to innovate, to shape the digital world is becoming accessible to anyone with a clear vision and the willingness to engage in a new kind of creative conversation.

Your ideas matter. Your perspective is valuable. Your creativity is needed. Whether you dream of building a simple utility, a beautiful online space, or the seed of the next big thing, the tools and techniques exist *now* to help you start that journey.

So, take a deep breath. Let go of the intimidation you might have felt about coding. Open your mind to a new way of thinking about software creation. It's time to unlock that inner coder you didn't know you had.

Welcome to the world of Vibe Coding. Let's start creating together.

CHAPTER 2: WHERE DID THIS VIBE COME FROM? (A QUICK HISTORY)

This Chapter Covers

- **Historical Context:** Vibe Coding is the latest step in a long history of making computer interaction easier (from punch cards to modern languages).
- **Evolution, Not Revolution:** Programming languages, tools (IDEs, libraries), and online communities gradually lowered barriers but still required significant coding skill.
- **The AI Breakthrough:** Recent Large Language Models (LLMs) are powerful enough to understand natural language *and* generate functional code, changing the game.
- **Emergence of the Practice:** People began building things conversationally with AI, focusing on the goal ("vibe") rather than just the code.
- **Naming the Vibe:** Andrej Karpathy coined/popularized the term "Vibe Coding" in early 2025, capturing this AI-driven, intuitive approach.
- **"Perfect Storm":** Vibe Coding took off due to mature LLMs, accessible tools, developer culture shifts, and high demand for digital creation (creator economy/no-code).
- **Current State:** It's a new, rapidly evolving field, shifting focus towards vision and guidance over deep technical expertise.

> *"If I have seen further it is by standing on the shoulders of Giants."*
>
> **- Isaac Newton**

In the last chapter, we introduced the exciting, almost magical concept of Vibe Coding – the idea that you can bring your digital ideas to life simply by talking to an Artificial Intelligence, guiding it through conversation and intuition. It sounds revolutionary, perhaps even futuristic. And in many ways, it is. But like most overnight sensations, Vibe Coding didn't just appear out of thin air. It's the culmination of a long, fascinating journey in how humans have learned to communicate with machines, a journey constantly driven by the desire to make creation easier, more accessible, and more powerful.

To truly appreciate *why* Vibe Coding is possible now, and why it feels so different, it helps to take a quick, non-technical peek back at how we got here. Don't worry, we won't get bogged down in complex timelines or technical jargon. Think of it as understanding the backstory of our incredibly helpful, code-writing AI apprentice. Where did it learn its skills? What paved the way for this new kind of creative partnership?

From Punch Cards to Plain English: The Long Quest for Easier Creation

Imagine the very earliest days of computing, back in the mid-20th century. Computers were colossal machines filling entire rooms, whirring and clicking, tended to by scientists in lab coats. Telling these machines what to do was an incredibly painstaking process. Programmers often had to physically rewire circuits or feed instructions into the machine using stacks of stiff paper cards with holes punched in specific patterns – punch cards.

Think about that for a second. Your brilliant idea for, say, calculating a trajectory or sorting data had to be translated into a precise sequence of holes on hundreds of cards. Make one mistake, punch one hole in the wrong place, and your entire program could fail, often without telling you why. It was meticulous, error-prone, and required immense patience and specialized knowledge. It was about as far from "coding by vibe" as you can possibly get! The communication barrier between human intent and machine execution was enormous.

Naturally, pioneers in computing knew there had to be a better way. The quest began almost immediately to create more human-friendly ways to instruct computers. This led to the development of the first **programming languages**.

Early languages, like Assembly language, were still quite cryptic, acting as a thin layer over the machine's raw instructions. It was better than punch cards, but still required programmers to think very much like the computer itself.

Then came a significant leap: **higher-level programming languages**. Names like FORTRAN (for scientists and engineers) and COBOL (for business applications) emerged. These languages allowed programmers to write instructions using words and symbols that were closer to human language and mathematical notation. Instead of manipulating memory addresses directly, you could write something like READ PRICE or COMPUTE TOTAL = PRICE * QUANTITY. This was a huge step! It allowed programmers to focus more on the *problem* they were trying to solve and less on the intricate details of the machine's hardware. The communication barrier was shrinking.

Over the following decades, this evolution continued at pace. New languages were invented, each often designed to be easier to learn, more powerful for specific tasks, or better suited for new types of computing (like the rise of personal computers, the internet, and mobile devices). Languages like C, C++, Java, Python, Ruby, and JavaScript became popular. Each generation aimed to abstract away more of the underlying complexity, allowing developers to express more complex ideas with less code and in ways that felt more intuitive.

Think of it like the evolution of writing itself. Early forms might have been complex pictograms or hieroglyphics, understood only by scribes. Later, alphabets emerged, making writing more accessible. Then came grammar, structure, and tools like dictionaries and thesauruses, further refining our ability to express complex thoughts clearly. Programming languages followed a similar path, constantly striving for greater clarity, power, and ease of expression.

Alongside the languages themselves, **tools** were developed to help programmers work more efficiently.

- **Compilers and Interpreters:** These act like translators, converting the human-readable code programmers write into the low-level instructions the computer actually understands.
- **Integrated Development Environments (IDEs):** These are like sophisticated workshops for programmers, providing text editors with features like syntax highlighting (coloring different parts of the code to make it easier to read), autocompletion (suggesting code as you type), and debugging tools (helping find and fix errors).
- **Libraries and Frameworks:** These are collections of pre-written code that handle common tasks. Instead of writing code from scratch to, say, create a button on a webpage or connect to a database, developers could use these libraries, saving enormous amounts of time and effort.
- **Online Communities and Resources:** Websites like Stack Overflow emerged, creating vast repositories of questions and answers where developers could find solutions to common problems and learn from each other. Copying and pasting snippets of code found online became a standard (and sometimes joked about) part of the development process.

All these advancements – better languages, helpful tools, shared knowledge – dramatically lowered the barrier to entry compared to the punch-card era. They made software development more productive and accessible to a wider range of people. Yet, even with these aids, traditional programming still required significant learning, logical thinking, attention to detail, and the ability to translate human ideas into the strict, unforgiving syntax that computers demand. The "Idea Graveyard" we talked about in Chapter 1 still claimed many potential creations. The process was much improved, but a fundamental gap remained for those without the time, inclination, or resources to master the craft of coding.

Enter the AI Revolution: When Machines Started Understanding Us

For decades, Artificial Intelligence was largely the stuff of science fiction or specialized academic research. Early AI systems could perform specific tasks, like playing chess or recognizing simple patterns, but they lacked the flexibility and nuanced understanding of human language needed to engage in complex, creative tasks like writing software based on a conversation.

Then, starting primarily in the late 2010s and exploding into public consciousness in the early 2020s, something remarkable happened: the rise of **Large Language Models (LLMs)**.

You've likely encountered these models through tools like ChatGPT, Anthropic's Claude, Google's Gemini, and others. What made these LLMs so different?

Without getting overly technical, it boils down to a few key breakthroughs:

1. **Massive Data:** These models were trained on truly colossal amounts of text and code scraped from the internet – books, articles, websites, and vast repositories of public software code. This gave them unprecedented exposure to the patterns, structures, nuances, and vocabulary of human language and programming languages.
2. **Advanced Algorithms (Transformers):** A new type of AI architecture, known as the "transformer," proved exceptionally good at understanding context and relationships between words in a sentence, even over long stretches of text. This allowed the models to grasp meaning and intent much more effectively than previous AI generations.
3. **Scale:** Simply put, these models are enormous, with billions or even trillions of parameters (think of these as the internal "knobs" the AI adjusts during learning). This sheer scale allows them to capture an incredible amount of complexity and subtlety.

The result was AI that could not only understand human language with surprising accuracy but also *generate* coherent, contextually relevant, and often creative text in response. People were stunned by their ability to write poems, draft emails, summarize complex documents, translate languages, and even generate computer code.

This last ability – generating code – was the crucial piece of the puzzle that paved the way for Vibe Coding. Suddenly, here was an AI that you could talk to in plain English, describe a programming task, and it could often write the necessary code, or at least provide a very good starting point.

The experience of interacting with these early code-generating LLMs was often startling, even for experienced programmers. You could ask it to "Write a Python function to read data from a CSV file and calculate the average of the 'Sales' column," and it would often produce perfectly functional code in seconds. You could describe a website layout using HTML and CSS, and it would generate the structure. You could paste in an error message you were stuck on, and it could often explain the problem and suggest a fix.

This wasn't just autocompletion or finding snippets on Stack Overflow. This felt different. It felt like having a conversation with an incredibly knowledgeable, albeit sometimes quirky, programming assistant. The AI wasn't just retrieving information; it was *synthesizing* it, *generating* novel solutions based on your specific request.

The "Aha!" Moment and the Birth of a Name

As these powerful LLMs became more accessible, often through simple chat interfaces, people naturally started experimenting. Developers began using them to speed up their work, automate tedious tasks, learn new languages, and brainstorm solutions. But something else started happening too. People *without* traditional coding backgrounds began poking at these tools, driven by curiosity and the desire to create.

They started asking things like, "Can you make me a simple website for my dog walking business?" or "How would I write a script to automatically rename all my photos?" And often, the AI would oblige, providing code that, perhaps with a bit of copying, pasting, and online searching, could actually *work*.

This experimentation created a buzz. A sense that the rules were changing. People were building things, sometimes complex things, by primarily *talking* to an AI. They weren't necessarily understanding every line of code generated, but they were achieving their desired outcomes through this iterative, conversational process. They were focusing on their goal, their vision, their "vibe," and letting the AI handle the heavy lifting of implementation.

It was into this environment of excitement, experimentation, and perhaps a touch of uncertainty, that the term "Vibe Coding" was formally introduced.

In **early 2025**, **Andrej Karpathy**, a highly respected computer scientist with influential roles at companies like OpenAI (one of the creators of GPT models) and Tesla, made waves with a social media post. He described a new way he was experimenting with building software, heavily relying on AI assistance. He wasn't just using AI for suggestions; he was letting it drive the process, accepting its code output, often without deep scrutiny, and guiding it primarily through high-level prompts and feedback on errors. He called this approach **"Vibe Coding."**

Karpathy's description captured the essence of what many were starting to experience: a state where you "fully give in to the vibes," embrace the AI's capabilities, and potentially even "forget that the code even exists," focusing instead on the iterative cycle of prompting, testing, and refining based on the outcome's feel and functionality. He framed it playfully, acknowledging the potential lack of deep understanding, but also highlighting the surprising effectiveness for certain tasks, like rapid prototyping or personal projects.

This wasn't necessarily Karpathy *inventing* the practice – people were already doing similar things. But by giving it a catchy, memorable name, and coming from such an influential figure in the AI world, his post acted as a catalyst. "Vibe Coding" suddenly had a label.

The term took off like wildfire within online tech communities – on Twitter (now X), Reddit forums like r/programming and r/ChatGPTCoding, tech blogs, and newsletters.

- Some developers embraced it, sharing stories of incredible productivity gains or how they built complex prototypes in record time.
- Others reacted with skepticism or even alarm, worrying about code quality, security risks, and the potential deskilling of programmers.
- Many were simply curious, asking "What is this 'vibe coding' everyone's talking about?"

Karpathy's post, and the name he coined, didn't create the underlying technology, but it perfectly captured the *zeitgeist* – the spirit of the times. It gave shape and identity to a new, slightly rebellious, AI-powered approach to creation that was emerging organically at the intersection of powerful language models and human ingenuity.

Why Now? The Perfect Storm for Creation

So, why did Vibe Coding emerge specifically in the mid-2020s? Why not earlier? It was the result of a "perfect storm" – a convergence of several key factors:

1. **Maturity of LLMs:** This is the most critical factor. As we discussed, the AI models simply weren't capable enough before. Earlier AI could handle narrow tasks, but the ability of models like GPT-4 and its contemporaries to understand nuanced natural language instructions and generate complex, functional code was the game-changer. They finally crossed a threshold where conversational interaction could yield meaningful software output.
2. **Accessibility of Tools:** These powerful LLMs weren't locked away in research labs. They were made available through relatively easy-to-use interfaces – web chatbots, APIs (Application Programming

Interfaces) that allowed other tools to integrate them, and dedicated platforms designed for AI-assisted coding (like Cursor or Replit's features). This widespread accessibility meant millions of people could experiment easily.

3. **Shift in Developer Culture:** The software development world has always been evolving. There was already a growing trend towards higher levels of abstraction (using frameworks and libraries to avoid repetitive coding) and a culture comfortable with leveraging online resources (like Stack Overflow). Vibe Coding felt, to some, like the next logical step in this evolution – outsourcing even more of the implementation details, this time to an AI.

4. **The Rise of the Creator Economy & No-Code:** Parallel trends like the creator economy and the success of no-code/low-code platforms had already highlighted a massive appetite among non-technical individuals to build their own digital presences, tools, and businesses. This audience was primed for a solution that offered even more flexibility and power than traditional no-code tools, without requiring them to become full-fledged programmers. Vibe Coding arrived at a time when the desire to create digitally was arguably at an all-time high.

It was the synergy of these factors – the raw capability of the AI, the ease of access to the tools, a developer culture open to new forms of assistance, and a large potential audience eager to create – that allowed the concept of Vibe Coding to take root and flourish so quickly. The "Aha!" moment wasn't just one person's realization, but a collective dawning across diverse communities that building software could fundamentally change.

A New Chapter in Creation (Still Being Written)

It's crucial to remember that Vibe Coding is incredibly new. We are witnessing the very beginning of this phenomenon. It's not a rigidly defined engineering methodology with decades of established best practices. It's more like a nascent movement, an evolving set of practices, and an ongoing conversation.

The tools are changing almost daily, becoming more powerful and integrated. The techniques for prompting and interacting effectively with AI are constantly being refined. The debates about its merits, risks, and long-term implications are lively and ongoing.

What does this mean for you, the creator eager to explore this space? It means you are stepping into a field that is dynamic, exciting, and still largely uncharted. It means that by learning about Vibe Coding now, you are positioning yourself at the forefront of a significant shift in digital creation.

It also means that having a guide – like this book aims to be – can be incredibly helpful. We can navigate the core principles, explore the essential tools, learn practical techniques, understand the potential pitfalls, and develop a mindset for creating effectively and responsibly in this new paradigm.

The history of computing has been a relentless march towards making it easier for humans to translate their ideas into functional reality. From punch cards to high-level languages, from command lines to graphical interfaces, each step has lowered barriers and unlocked creativity. The arrival of capable, code-generating AI represents perhaps the most dramatic leap yet in this journey. It opens the door for a future where the primary constraint on digital creation might not be technical skill, but the clarity and power of your vision.

The "vibe" has arrived. Now, let's learn how to work with it.

CHAPTER 3: OKAY, BUT WHAT IS VIBE CODING, REALLY?

This Chapter Covers

- **Core Idea:** Creative partnership: You direct (natural language), AI builds (code).
- **Process Loop:** Describe -> AI Codes -> Test -> Refine via feedback.
- **Your Role:** Director/Guide (vision, communication, testing).
- **vs. Traditional Coding:** Faster iteration, uses communication > coding skill, less direct code control.
- **vs. No-Code:** Language-based (flexible/unpredictable) vs. Visual blocks (limited/predictable).
- **The "Vibe":** Leverages intuition, rapid experimentation, user experience focus.
- **In Essence:** A new way to create software via AI conversation, prioritizing vision & iteration.

"Simplicity is about subtracting the obvious and adding the meaningful."

- John Maeda

In the previous chapters, we've danced around the edges of Vibe Coding. We've felt the frustration it aims to solve, glimpsed its historical context, and shared a story of its empowering potential. We've called it revolutionary, almost magical. But now, it's time to pull back the curtain a little further. What *exactly* is happening when you're "Vibe Coding"? What does the process look like, feel like, and how does it fundamentally differ from other ways of creating software?

Understanding this core concept clearly, without needing a computer science degree, is key to unlocking its power for your own creative projects. Forget the intimidating jargon and complex theories for a moment. Let's break down Vibe Coding into its essential parts, using simple language and relatable ideas. At its heart, it's a new kind of creative partnership between you and an Artificial Intelligence.

The Core Process: A Conversation with Your AI Co-Creator

Imagine you have an idea for a simple mobile app: a "Mindful Moment Reminder." You want it to send you a gentle notification three times a day, prompting you to take a deep breath and be present for just 60 seconds. How would you build this using Vibe Coding? The process generally unfolds in a conversational, iterative loop:

Step 1: Describe Your Vision (The Spark of Intent)

This is where it all begins. You don't start by sketching flowcharts or writing complex specifications (unless you want to!). You start by *talking* to your AI assistant, typically through a chat interface, much like you'd brief a collaborator. You use plain English to describe what you want.

- **You might say:** "I want to create a simple mobile app called 'Mindful Moment Reminder'. Its main purpose is to send a notification to the user three times a day – maybe morning, afternoon, and evening. The notification should just say something like 'Time for a mindful moment. Take 60 seconds to breathe.'"

Notice how this is focused on the *what* and the *why*. You're explaining the goal, the core functionality, and even suggesting the user-facing text. You're not worrying about *how* the notifications will be scheduled or delivered technically. You're articulating your intent. Clarity is helpful here – the clearer you can describe your vision, the better the AI can understand and assist. You might also specify the platform (e.g., "make it for iOS") or any initial design ideas ("use a calm blue color scheme").

Step 2: The AI Generates Code (The Initial Creation)

This is where the AI steps in as your co-creator. Based on your description, the Large Language Model (LLM) accesses its vast knowledge of programming languages, patterns, and common app structures. It processes your request and starts generating the actual computer code needed to build the initial version of your app.

- **The AI might respond:** "Okay, I can help with that. I'll set up a basic structure for an iOS app using Swift. I'll include a simple interface and the logic to schedule three daily notifications with the text you provided. Here's the initial code:" [AI would then present code snippets or files].

This step can feel quite magical, especially the first few times. You've simply described an idea, and now you're seeing potentially functional code appear. However, it's crucial to manage expectations. The AI's first attempt might not be perfect. It might have misunderstood something, made assumptions, or generated code that has subtle bugs. Think of this as the first draft, the initial sketch.

Step 3: You Test and Evaluate (The Reality Check)

Now the ball is back in your court. The AI has produced something, but does it actually work? Does it match your vision? You need to test it.

How you test depends on the tool you're using. Some platforms might let you run the app directly in a simulator or preview window. In other cases, you might need to copy the code into an appropriate environment (something we'll cover in later chapters on tools).

- **You run the prototype:** You might find the app installs, but maybe the notifications aren't appearing. Or perhaps they appear, but the timing is wrong. Maybe the interface looks bare or not quite right.

This testing phase isn't about understanding the code itself (though you might start picking things up!). It's about observing the *behavior* of the app. Does it *do* what you asked it to do? Does it *look* and *feel* the way you intended? You are evaluating the output against your original vision and the desired "vibe."

Step 4: Provide Feedback and Refine (The Iterative Loop)

Based on your testing, you go back to the AI with feedback. This is where the conversational aspect really shines. You tell the AI what's working, what's not, and what you want to change.

- **You might say:** "Thanks! The app seems to load, but I didn't receive any notifications. Can you check the notification scheduling code?"
- **Or:** "The notifications are working now, great! But can we change the times? I'd prefer 9 AM, 1 PM, and 8 PM."
- **Or:** "Could you add a simple button on the main screen that says 'Request an Extra Moment'? When tapped, it should send one immediate notification."
- **Or even aesthetic feedback:** "The background is plain white. Can you make it a soft, calming gradient of blue?"

You describe the discrepancies, the desired changes, or the new features in natural language. The AI takes your feedback, attempts to understand it, and generates updated code or suggests modifications. You then test again.

This cycle – **Describe -> AI Codes -> Test -> Refine -> Describe -> AI Codes...** – is the fundamental engine of Vibe Coding. You iterate, gradually shaping the application through conversation, guiding the AI closer and closer to your goal. Each loop might fix a bug, add a feature, or improve the user experience. It's a dynamic dance between your intent and the AI's execution.

Your role in this process is absolutely crucial. You are not passively receiving code; you are actively **directing** the creation. You are the visionary, the guide, the tester, and the quality controller, all rolled into one. The AI is your incredibly fast, knowledgeable, but sometimes literal-minded assistant.

Your Role: The Director, Not Just the Builder

To truly grasp the shift Vibe Coding represents, let's lean into an analogy. Think about making a movie.

- **The Director:** The director holds the overall vision for the film. They understand the story, the characters, the desired mood, the target audience. They don't necessarily need to know how to operate the camera, design the lighting rig, build the sets, or apply the makeup themselves. Their job is to communicate their vision effectively to the experts in each department (cinematographer, lighting designer, set decorator, makeup artist) and guide their work. The director reviews the daily footage (the "dailies"), provides feedback ("I want a tighter shot here," "Let's make the lighting moodier," "That line reading felt flat"), and makes creative decisions to ensure the final film aligns with their vision. They are the ultimate arbiter of the "vibe" of the movie.
- **The Crew:** The crew members are the specialists. The cinematographer knows cameras and lenses, the set decorator understands props and furniture, the actors embody the characters. They take the director's high-level instructions and use their specific skills and tools to execute them.

In the Vibe Coding scenario, **you are the Director.** Your app idea is your movie concept. Your understanding of the user, the desired experience, the overall feel – that's your directorial vision.

The **AI is your multi-talented Crew.** It's the cinematographer, the set builder, the editor, all rolled into one incredibly fast assistant. It knows the "technical" aspects – the programming languages, the standard structures, the common ways to implement features.

Your job as the Vibe Coding Director involves:

1. **Communicating the Vision:** Clearly explaining the concept, the features, the target user, and the desired "vibe" of your app (your prompts).
2. **Delegating Tasks:** Asking the AI to implement specific features or make specific changes ("Add a login screen," "Change the color palette").
3. **Reviewing the Dailies:** Testing the app or website the AI generates to see if it works correctly and matches your intent.
4. **Providing Feedback:** Telling the AI what needs to be adjusted, fixed, or added based on your review.

5. **Maintaining Cohesion:** Ensuring that all the different parts the AI builds work together harmoniously towards your overall goal.

Just like a film director doesn't need to be an expert camera operator, you, as the Vibe Coding Director, don't need to be an expert programmer. Your core skills are **vision, communication, evaluation, and iterative guidance.** You leverage the AI's technical execution capabilities to bring your creative vision to life.

Let's briefly consider other analogies:

- **The Architect:** An architect designs a building based on the client's needs and aesthetic desires. They create blueprints and models (the vision). They don't physically lay the bricks or install the plumbing, but they communicate the design to the engineers and construction crew (the AI) and oversee the building process, ensuring it matches the plans and quality standards.
- **The Chef:** A head chef designs a menu and specific dishes (the vision). They instruct their team of sous chefs and line cooks (the AI) on how to prepare the ingredients and assemble the plates. The head chef tastes the results, provides feedback ("Needs more salt," "Cook this longer," "Plate it more elegantly"), and ensures the final dish meets their standards, without necessarily chopping every vegetable themselves.

All these analogies highlight the shift: Vibe Coding elevates your role from direct, hands-on implementation to one of **strategic guidance, creative direction, and quality control, mediated through conversation with an AI.**

How Vibe Coding Differs: Standing Apart from the Familiar

To solidify our understanding, let's explicitly contrast Vibe Coding with the two main alternatives we discussed in Chapter 1: Traditional Coding and No-Code/Low-Code platforms. Understanding these differences helps clarify Vibe Coding's unique position, its strengths, and its potential weaknesses.

Vibe Coding vs. Traditional Coding

This is perhaps the most significant contrast. While both aim to create software, the process, required skills, and mindset are vastly different.

- **The Core Activity:**
  - *Traditional Coding:* Manually writing precise instructions line-by-line in a specific programming language (like Python, JavaScript, Swift). Requires deep knowledge of syntax, logic, algorithms, and data structures.

- o *Vibe Coding:* Describing desired outcomes and features in natural language and guiding an AI that generates the code. Relies more on communication and evaluation skills.
- **Required Knowledge:**
  - o *Traditional Coding:* Extensive knowledge of one or more programming languages, development tools, frameworks, and often computer science fundamentals. Steep learning curve.
  - o *Vibe Coding:* Primarily requires a clear vision, good communication skills (for prompting), the ability to test and evaluate results, and a willingness to iterate. Technical knowledge is helpful but not strictly necessary to get started. Much lower initial barrier.
- **The Process & Workflow:**
  - o *Traditional Coding:* Often involves detailed planning, designing architecture, writing code meticulously, debugging logically (tracing errors through code), and rigorous testing. Can be more linear, though agile methods incorporate iteration.
  - o *Vibe Coding:* Highly iterative and exploratory. Relies on a rapid loop of prompting, generating, testing, and refining. Debugging often involves describing the problem back to the AI rather than analyzing the code directly. Can feel more organic or sometimes chaotic.
- **Speed & Effort:**
  - o *Traditional Coding:* Can be time-consuming, especially for complex features or when dealing with bugs. Requires significant focused effort.
  - o *Vibe Coding:* Can be dramatically faster for generating initial prototypes, boilerplate code, or standard features. The AI handles the bulk of the typing. Effort shifts from implementation to guidance and testing.
- **Control vs. Abstraction:**
  - o *Traditional Coding:* Offers maximum control. The developer understands (or *should* understand) every line of code and how it works.
  - o *Vibe Coding:* Involves a higher level of abstraction. You control the direction, but you delegate the implementation details to the AI. You might not understand precisely *how* the AI generated code works internally. This is both a source of its power (speed, accessibility) and its potential risks (hidden bugs, maintenance challenges if you don't understand the code).
- **Debugging:**

- *Traditional Coding:* Requires logical problem-solving, reading code, using debugging tools to step through execution and identify the root cause of errors.
- *Vibe Coding:* Often involves describing the symptoms of the error to the AI ("When I click the save button, the app crashes") and asking it to propose a fix. It's more conversational troubleshooting than deep analysis. This can be faster for simple issues but potentially frustrating for complex bugs the AI can't easily grasp.

- **Mindset:**
  - *Traditional Coding:* Emphasizes precision, logic, control, structure, and deep understanding.
  - *Vibe Coding:* Emphasizes vision, communication, iteration, intuition, rapid experimentation, and focusing on the end-user experience or "vibe."

It's crucial to state that Vibe Coding doesn't necessarily *replace* traditional coding. Traditional coding remains essential for building complex, reliable, high-performance systems where deep understanding and control are paramount. Rather, Vibe Coding emerges as a *different* way to create, particularly powerful for rapid prototyping, building simpler applications, automating tasks, and empowering individuals who wouldn't otherwise engage in software development. It's adding a new, highly accessible tool to the creator's toolkit.

Vibe Coding vs. No-Code/Low-Code Platforms

On the surface, Vibe Coding might seem similar to No-Code/Low-Code tools, as both aim to lower the technical barrier to software creation. However, their approach and capabilities differ significantly.

- **Interaction Model:**
  - *No-Code/Low-Code:* Primarily rely on **visual interfaces**. Users drag and drop pre-built components (buttons, forms, data tables), connect them visually, and configure their properties through menus and settings panels. Think building with digital Lego blocks.
  - *Vibe Coding:* Primarily relies on **natural language interaction**. Users type or speak instructions (prompts) to an AI, which then generates the underlying code. Think having a conversation with your builder.
- **Flexibility & Customization:**
  - *No-Code/Low-Code:* Offer speed and ease for standard tasks defined by the platform's components. However, flexibility can be limited. If you need a feature or interaction not

supported by the available blocks, you might hit a wall or need to resort to custom code injections (moving into "low-code").

- o *Vibe Coding:* Potentially offers greater flexibility. Because the AI generates actual code, it *could* theoretically implement more custom logic or unique interface elements based on your description. However, this flexibility comes with less predictability – the AI might misunderstand complex requests or generate flawed code.

- **Learning Curve:**
  - o *No-Code/Low-Code:* While avoiding traditional code, these platforms have their own interfaces, concepts, and limitations that users need to learn. The learning curve is generally lower than traditional coding but still exists.
  - o *Vibe Coding:* Leverages existing natural language skills. The primary new skill to learn is **effective prompting** – how to communicate clearly and guide the AI efficiently. There's also the process of learning how to test and iterate with the AI's output.

- **Transparency & Control:**
  - o *No-Code/Low-Code:* Often provide a clear visual representation of the application's structure and logic. What you see is generally what you get. You have direct control over configuring the available components.
  - o *Vibe Coding:* The underlying code generated by the AI can be complex and potentially opaque to a non-technical user. While you control the *direction* via prompts, you have less direct control over the *implementation details* unless you choose to dive into the generated code. Predictability can also be lower; the same prompt might occasionally yield slightly different results from the AI.

- **Output:**
  - o *No-Code/Low-Code:* Typically produce applications locked into the platform's ecosystem, though some offer code export options (often complex).
  - o *Vibe Coding:* Directly generates source code (HTML, CSS, JavaScript, Python, etc.). This code *could* potentially be taken and used outside the initial AI tool, although understanding and managing it might require technical skills.

Think of it this way: No-Code platforms provide a curated set of high-quality, predictable building blocks and a visual assembly line. Vibe Coding provides a highly skilled but sometimes unpredictable craftsperson (the AI) who can theoretically build almost anything you describe, but requires careful direction and quality control.

Both approaches are valuable tools for democratizing creation. No-Code excels at rapidly building standard applications with predictable results. Vibe Coding offers a different path, potentially more flexible and conversational, allowing creation through natural language, but requiring a different set of skills focused on communication, iteration, and evaluation.

The "Vibe" in Vibe Coding: Intuition, Iteration, and Feel

We've used the word "vibe" quite a bit, referencing the term coined by Andrej Karpathy. But what does it really mean in this context beyond just being a catchy name? It points to several key aspects of this development style that resonate particularly well with creative individuals:

1. **Embracing Intuition:** Traditional programming often demands rigorous logic and planning upfront. Vibe Coding allows more room for intuition – your gut feeling about what will work for the user, what looks good, or what feels right. You can try things out quickly based on a hunch. If you have a background in design, art, writing, or any field where aesthetic sense and user empathy are important, Vibe Coding allows you to lead with those strengths. You can prompt the AI: "Make the design feel more welcoming," or "Simplify this section to make it less overwhelming," guiding the development based on your intuitive understanding of the desired experience.

2. **Rapid Iteration and Experimentation:** The speed at which AI can generate code enables incredibly fast iteration cycles. You can have an idea, prompt the AI, see a result, and refine it within minutes, not hours or days. This allows for rapid experimentation. Don't like the blue background? Ask for green. Want to try a different layout? Describe it. This quick feedback loop keeps creative momentum going. It aligns with the way many creative processes work – sketching, refining, trying variations, exploring possibilities without huge upfront commitments. You can "fail fast" – if an idea doesn't work visually or functionally, you find out quickly and can pivot without having invested days of manual coding.

3. **Focusing on the Feel and Experience:** Especially in the early stages, Vibe Coding encourages focusing on the overall "feel" – the user experience, the aesthetics, the core value proposition – rather than getting bogged down in low-level implementation details. Does the app *feel* responsive? Is the website *easy* to navigate? Does the tool *solve the user's problem* effectively? You're directing based on the desired qualities of the final product as experienced by a human, letting the AI worry about the underlying technical mechanics. This allows creators to stay closer to their original vision and user-centric goals.

4. **Working with Ambiguity (Initially):** While clear prompts are generally better, Vibe Coding allows you to start with a slightly fuzzier vision and refine it through interaction. You might not know

exactly how a feature should work technically, but you can describe the user's goal and see what the AI suggests. This exploratory approach can be very powerful for innovation, allowing ideas to evolve organically during the creation process.

5. **A Different Kind of "Flow":** Programmers often talk about entering a "flow state" – deep concentration while solving complex logical problems and writing code. Vibe Coding offers a different kind of flow, one based on conversation, rapid feedback, and creative direction. It can feel less like solitary deep work and more like an energetic brainstorming and co-creation session with your AI partner.

This "vibe" aspect is not about being sloppy or ignoring details entirely. It's about shifting the *focus*, especially early on, towards the experiential and intuitive aspects of creation, leveraging the AI's speed to explore and refine rapidly based on that feeling and vision. It makes the process feel less like rigid engineering and more like sculpting or directing – shaping the outcome through iterative adjustments guided by your sense of what works.

Putting It All Together

So, what is Vibe Coding, really?

It's a process where you use natural language to describe your software ideas to an AI, which generates the code.

It's a role where you act as the Director – guiding the AI, testing the results, and providing feedback through an iterative conversation.

It's a contrast to traditional coding (which requires deep technical skill and manual implementation) and No-Code tools (which use visual builders and pre-defined components).

It's a mindset that embraces intuition, rapid iteration, and focusing on the overall feel and user experience, leveraging AI speed to explore possibilities quickly.

It's new, it's evolving, and it's potentially game-changing for anyone who has ever had a brilliant digital idea but felt locked out by the technical barriers. It's not a replacement for all forms of software development, and it comes with its own set of challenges and responsibilities (which we'll explore thoroughly). But it represents a powerful new pathway for creation, one that puts your vision and your voice at the center of the process.

Now that we have a clearer picture of what Vibe Coding is, let's move on to meeting the specific AI tools that make this all possible.

CHAPTER 4: MEET YOUR AI CO-CREATORS: TOOLS FOR VIBING

This Chapter Covers

- **Focus:** Introduces accessible AI tools ("Co-Creators") for Vibe Coding beginners.
- **Chatbots (e.g., ChatGPT):** Easy start via chat; good for snippets/ideas; needs separate testing.
- **Online Platforms (e.g., Replit):** All-in-one web environment (code, test, AI); streamlines web projects.
- **Editor Plugins (e.g., Copilot):** Deeper AI integration in code editors; more technical; potential next step.
- **Core AI Abilities:** Understand language, generate/explain/debug code, brainstorm.
- **Getting Started:** Begin with chatbots or online platforms; experiment.

"Start where you are. Use what you have. Do what you can."

- Arthur Ashe

In the last chapter, we defined Vibe Coding as a dynamic conversation, an iterative dance between your vision and an AI's ability to generate code. You are the Director, setting the scene, guiding the action, and ensuring the final product matches your creative intent. But every director needs a capable crew, the talented specialists who handle the technical execution. In the world of Vibe Coding, your crew consists of powerful Artificial Intelligence tools specifically designed or adept at understanding language and generating software.

Think of these tools not as cold, complex pieces of technology, but as your **AI Co-Creators** or **Digital Assistants**. They are the incredibly knowledgeable, lightning-fast partners you'll be collaborating with. Just like any collaborator, they have strengths, quirks, and preferred ways of working. Getting to know them, understanding what they do best, and learning how to interact with them effectively is the next crucial step in your Vibe Coding journey.

The landscape of AI tools is vast and evolving at breakneck speed. New players emerge, existing ones get smarter, and capabilities expand constantly. It can feel overwhelming! But don't worry. For our purposes – empowering non-technical creators to start Vibe Coding – we can focus on a few key categories and specific tools that are particularly accessible and effective for beginners.

Our goal in this chapter is not to provide an exhaustive technical manual for every tool under the sun. Instead, we want to introduce you to the main players you're likely to encounter, explain *what* they do in simple terms, give you a feel for *how* you might use them in your creative process, and help you feel comfortable exploring them. We'll focus on tools that don't require you to already be a coding expert.

Remember the core Vibe Coding loop: **Describe -> AI Codes -> Test -> Refine**. The tools we'll discuss are designed to facilitate this loop, acting as the engine that translates your descriptions into code and helps you refine the results.

Let's meet your potential AI co-creators.

Category 1: The Conversational Consultants (General Chatbots like ChatGPT & Claude)

Perhaps the most familiar and easily accessible entry point into AI-powered creation are the general-purpose AI chatbots that have taken the world by storm. Tools like OpenAI's **ChatGPT** and Anthropic's **Claude** are prime examples.

Claud interface

While designed for a wide range of conversational tasks – answering questions, writing emails, summarizing text, brainstorming ideas – these chatbots are also surprisingly adept at understanding programming concepts and generating code. They represent an excellent starting point for Vibe Coding because their interface is incredibly simple: it's just a chat window. If you can type a message, you can start interacting with these AI assistants.

- **The Interface:** Imagine a simple messaging app. You type your request (your prompt) into a text box at the bottom, hit send, and the AI's response appears in the chat history above. It's intuitive and requires virtually no technical setup.

- **What They Do Well for Vibe Coding:**
  - **Understanding Natural Language:** They excel at interpreting your plain English descriptions of what you want to build. You can explain your idea conversationally.
  - **Generating Code Snippets:** They are great at writing specific pieces of code based on your requests. Need the HTML for a contact form? Want a JavaScript function to calculate something? Ask, and they can often generate it instantly.
  - **Explaining Code:** If the AI generates code you don't understand (which will happen!), you can ask it to explain what the code does, line by line, in simple terms. This makes them fantastic learning companions.
  - **Debugging Assistance (Conceptual):** If you encounter an error message when trying to run code (perhaps code the AI generated earlier, or code you found elsewhere), you can often paste the error message into the chat and ask the AI what might be wrong and how to fix it. It can act like a knowledgeable tutor, helping you troubleshoot.
  - **Brainstorming and Ideation:** Stuck on how a feature should work or how your app should be structured? You can brainstorm with the chatbot, asking for ideas, suggestions, or different ways to approach a problem.
- **How You Might Use Them (Hypothetical Scenarios):**
  - **Scenario A: Building a Basic Webpage Element:**
    - *You:* "Can you give me the HTML and CSS code for a simple button that says 'Learn More' and has a blue background with white text?"
    - *ChatGPT/Claude:* "Sure, here is the HTML and CSS code for that button: [Provides code snippets]."
    - *You:* "Thanks! How can I make the corners slightly rounded?"
    - *ChatGPT/Claude:* "You can add the border-radius property in the CSS. Here's the updated CSS: [Provides updated code]."
  - **Scenario B: Understanding an Error:**
    - *You:* "I'm trying to run this JavaScript code you gave me earlier, but I'm getting this error in the console: TypeError: Cannot read property 'value' of null. What does that mean?"
    - *ChatGPT/Claude:* "That error usually means you're trying to access a property (like .value) on something that doesn't exist or hasn't been found (it's null). This often happens if you're trying to get the value from an HTML element using its ID, but there's no element with that ID on the page, or the script is running before

the element has loaded..." [Provides further explanation and possible fixes].

- o **Scenario C: Planning a Feature:**
  - *You:* "I'm building a simple recipe app. I need a way for users to save their favorite recipes. What are some simple ways I could implement that?"
  - *ChatGPT/Claude:* "There are several ways! For simplicity, you could: 1. Use the browser's local storage to save a list of favorite recipe IDs directly on the user's device. 2. If users have accounts, you could add a 'favorites' field to their user profile in a database..." [Explains pros and cons of each].

- **Potential Limitations:**
  - o **Managing Large Projects:** While great for snippets and individual features, managing an entire complex application purely within a chatbot interface can become cumbersome. You'll likely be copying and pasting code into separate files or other tools.
  - o **Context Window:** Chatbots have a limit to how much of the previous conversation they can "remember" (their "context window"). In very long conversations about a complex project, they might start to forget earlier details or instructions, requiring you to remind them.
  - o **Direct Execution:** You typically can't *run* the code directly within the chatbot itself. You need to take the code it generates and run it elsewhere (like in a browser, a code editor, or an online platform) to test it. This adds an extra step to the Test -> Refine loop.

- **The Feeling:** Using a tool like ChatGPT or Claude for Vibe Coding often feels like having a very patient, knowledgeable, and sometimes overly literal tutor or assistant by your side. It's conversational, accessible, and great for learning and generating specific pieces of your project. It's an excellent place to start experimenting with prompts and seeing AI generate code in response to your ideas.

Category 2: The Integrated Online Workshop (Platforms like Replit)

While chatbots are fantastic conversational partners, sometimes you want a more integrated environment – a place where you can not only talk to the AI and get code generated but also easily edit that code, run it, test it, and even potentially host your finished project, all in one place. This is where online coding platforms with built-in AI features shine. A prominent example often mentioned in the context of accessible, AI-powered development is **Replit**.

Think of Replit (and similar platforms) as an online workshop or studio, accessible entirely through your web browser. There's typically nothing to install on your computer. You sign up, create a new project (often called a "Repl"), and you get a coding environment ready to go.

- **The Interface:** These platforms usually present a more structured interface than a simple chatbot. You might see:
  - A file explorer on the left, showing the files that make up your project.
  - A central area for editing code.
  - A console or output window on the right or bottom, where you can see results, error messages, or run commands.
  - Crucially, integrated AI features – perhaps a dedicated chat panel for talking to an AI assistant, or AI suggestions appearing directly in the code editor.

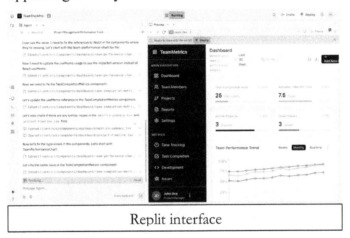

Replit interface

- **What They Do Well for Vibe Coding:**
  - **All-in-One Environment:** They combine code editing, file management, execution (running your code), and AI assistance in one browser tab. This significantly streamlines the Vibe Coding loop, especially the "Test" phase.
  - **Ease of Setup:** You can often start coding in various languages (HTML/CSS/JS for websites, Python for scripts, etc.) with a single click, without worrying about complex local installations or configurations. This is a massive advantage for beginners.
  - **Direct Code Execution & Testing:** You can typically run your web app or script directly within the platform and see the results immediately in a preview window or console. This makes the Test -> Refine cycle much faster than copying code from a separate chatbot.
  - **Integrated AI Assistants:** Platforms like Replit often have AI features specifically designed for their environment. This might include an "Agent" that can attempt to build entire projects from a description, or an "Assistant" in a chat panel

that understands the context of your project files and can help generate, explain, or debug code relevant to what you're working on.

- o **Collaboration & Sharing:** Many platforms make it easy to share your projects with others for feedback or collaboration.
- o **Deployment (Hosting):** Often, these platforms offer simple ways to deploy your project, making your website or app live on the internet with just a few clicks.

- **How You Might Use Them (Hypothetical Workflow for the 'Mindful Moment Reminder'):**
    - o **Start Project:** You go to Replit, click "Create Repl," choose a template (maybe "HTML, CSS, JS" if it were a web version, or a relevant mobile template if available).
    - o **Initial Prompt (AI Panel):** You open the integrated AI chat panel and type your initial description: "Create the basic structure for a 'Mindful Moment Reminder' app. It needs to schedule three daily notifications..."
    - o **AI Generates Files:** The AI might directly create or modify the necessary files (e.g., index.html, style.css, script.js) within your project structure.
    - o **Run & Test:** You click the "Run" button. A preview window might pop up showing the basic interface, or you might check the console for confirmation about notification scheduling (depending on the app type). You notice the notifications aren't working yet.
    - o **Refine (AI Panel):** You go back to the AI chat: "The notifications don't seem to be working. Can you check the code in script.js?"
    - o **AI Modifies Code:** The AI analyzes the code *within your project context* and suggests or applies changes directly to the script.js file.
    - o **Run & Test Again:** You click "Run" again. This time, maybe you see confirmation or the notifications start working in a simulator.
    - o **Add Features (AI Panel):** "Okay, now add a button with the text 'Request an Extra Moment' to the index.html file and make it trigger an immediate notification using JavaScript in script.js."
    - o **AI Modifies Files:** The AI updates both the HTML and JavaScript files.
    - o **Run & Test...** and so the iterative loop continues, all within the same browser tab.
- **Potential Limitations:**
    - o **Platform Lock-in (Potential):** While you often get standard code, the integrated AI features and deployment options might work best within that specific platform's ecosystem.

- o **Resource Limits:** Free tiers usually have limitations on computing power, storage, or network usage, which might be a factor for larger or more demanding applications.
- o **Interface Complexity:** While easier than setting up a local environment, the multi-panel interface of an online IDE can still be slightly more intimidating for absolute beginners than a simple chatbot window.
- **The Feeling:** Using an integrated online platform like Replit for Vibe Coding feels like stepping into a fully equipped digital workshop. Everything you need is at your fingertips – the materials (files), the tools (editor, runner), and your AI assistant, all working together seamlessly. It significantly speeds up the crucial testing part of the Vibe Coding loop and makes the whole process feel more contained and efficient, especially for web-based projects.

Category 3: The Embedded Assistants (Editor Plugins like Copilot & Cursor)

There's a third category worth mentioning briefly, although it often requires a bit more technical familiarity. These are AI assistants designed to work *inside* traditional code editors – the software many professional developers use on their computers (like Visual Studio Code, Sublime Text, etc.). Examples include **GitHub Copilot** and dedicated AI-first editors like **Cursor**.

- **GitHub Copilot:** This tool primarily works like an incredibly smart autocomplete. As you start typing code (or even comments describing what you want to do), Copilot suggests entire lines or blocks of code to complete your thought. It learns from the context of your project. While powerful for speeding up manual coding, it's slightly different from the core Vibe Coding loop, which often starts with a natural language prompt rather than starting to type code. However, a vibe coder might use Copilot if they decide to manually tweak the AI-generated code.
- **Cursor:** This is a more recent development – a code editor built *specifically* with AI integration at its core. It allows you to chat with an AI that understands your entire codebase, highlight code and ask questions about it, generate code from prompts directly within the editor, and automatically apply AI-suggested fixes. It blends the conversational aspect of chatbots with the structured environment of a code editor, making it very well-suited for a Vibe Coding workflow, potentially offering more power and context awareness than a general chatbot. Andrej Karpathy himself mentioned using Cursor in his early descriptions of Vibe Coding.
- **Why We Mention Them Briefly:** While powerful, these tools generally require you to install and configure a code editor on your computer, which can be a hurdle for non-technical beginners. Their

interfaces are designed for developers and might feel complex initially. We include them here for context, as you might hear about them, and they could represent a potential "next step" if you become more comfortable and want deeper integration or control than web-based platforms offer. For starting out, the chatbots and online platforms are usually more immediately accessible.

Core Capabilities: What Your AI Co-Creator Can Do For You

Regardless of whether you choose a chatbot, an online platform, or eventually explore editor integrations, the underlying AI engines powering these tools offer a set of core capabilities that are invaluable for Vibe Coding:

1. **Understanding Your Instructions (Natural Language Processing):** This is the foundation. You speak or type in plain English (or another language), describing what you want, and the AI interprets your intent. This ability to bridge the gap between human language and computer code is what makes Vibe Coding possible.
   o *Example:* You say, "Create a list of tasks with checkboxes." The AI understands you need HTML elements, perhaps some styling, and maybe JavaScript to handle checking items off.
2. **Generating Code (Code Synthesis):** Based on its understanding, the AI writes the code. This can range from single lines or functions to entire files or basic project structures. It draws on its training data of countless programming examples.
   o *Example:* Following the previous prompt, the AI generates the necessary HTML <ul>, <li>, and <input type="checkbox"> tags, along with basic CSS for layout.
3. **Explaining Code (Demystification):** This is incredibly useful for learning and building confidence. If the AI generates code that looks like gibberish to you, you can ask it to explain.
   o *Example:* You ask, "What does this line document.getElementById('taskInput').value; do?" The AI explains that it finds an HTML element with the ID 'taskInput' (likely a text box) and gets the text value the user typed into it.
4. **Debugging Assistance (Troubleshooting):** When things go wrong, the AI can help diagnose problems. You describe the error message or the unexpected behavior.
   o *Example:* You say, "The tasks aren't being saved when I close the page. How can I fix that?" The AI might explain that you need to use local storage and provide the JavaScript code to save and load the tasks.
5. **Brainstorming and Suggesting Ideas (Creative Partnership):** Don't underestimate the AI's ability to be a creative partner. If you're unsure how to approach something, ask for suggestions.
   o *Example:* "I want to add reminders to my task list app. What are some ways I could do that?" The AI might suggest using

browser notifications, integrating with calendar APIs, or simply highlighting overdue tasks visually.

Mastering Vibe Coding involves learning how to effectively leverage *all* these capabilities through skillful prompting and iterative refinement.

Choosing Your First Co-Creator & Taking the Plunge

So, with these options laid out, where should you begin? There's no single right answer, as it depends on your comfort level and the type of project you have in mind. Here's a simple suggestion:

- **For Absolute Beginners (Just Exploring):** Start with one of the **General Chatbots** (ChatGPT or Claude). Their simple chat interface is the least intimidating. You can immediately start experimenting with prompts, asking questions, generating code snippets, and getting a feel for the conversational interaction without any setup. Focus on understanding the Describe -> AI Codes part of the loop.
- **For Building Your First Simple Web Project:** Consider trying an **Online Platform** like **Replit**. The integrated environment makes the Test -> Refine part of the loop much smoother, as you can run your code instantly. The ease of setup for web technologies (HTML, CSS, JS) is a huge plus.
- **If You're Curious About Code Structure:** If you find yourself wanting to look at the generated code more closely or start making small manual edits, exploring an **Online Platform** with a built-in editor or eventually trying an AI-first editor like **Cursor** might be logical next steps.

The most important thing is to **start experimenting**. Don't feel pressured to choose the "perfect" tool right away. Pick one that seems accessible, sign up (many have free tiers), and try giving it a simple task related to an idea you have.

- Ask it to generate the HTML for a webpage title.
- Ask it to write a short Python script to print "Hello, World!"
- Ask it to explain a simple coding concept you've heard of.

Treat it like meeting a new collaborator. Be clear in your requests, be patient if it misunderstands, provide feedback, and see what you can create together. The tools are ready and waiting. They are your co-creators, your digital assistants, ready to help you bridge the gap between imagination and implementation.

In the next chapter, we'll dive into the practical heart of Vibe Coding: building your very first application step-by-step through this conversational, AI-assisted process. Get ready to bring your ideas to life!

CHAPTER 5: FROM IDEA TO APP: YOUR FIRST VIBE CODING PROJECT

This Chapter Covers

- **Focus:** Walkthrough building a "Movie Watchlist" app via Vibe Coding (process, no code shown).
- **Assumed Tool:** Online Platform (e.g., Replit).
- **Process Steps:**
  1. intent & vibe.
  2. Prompt AI for structure, then functionality (add, style).
  3. Test & refine iteratively.
  4. Add features (e.g., "watched" button/action).
  5. Troubleshoot errors via conversation (e.g., fix saving).
  6. Refine aesthetics ("Vibe Check").
  7. Accept when Version 1 goals are met.
- **Roles:** You = Director (vision, prompts, test); AI = Crew (codes, fixes).
- **Goal:** Demonstrate the conversational workflow to build confidence.

"The journey of a thousand miles begins with a single step."

- Lao Tzu

Okay, let's embark on building our very first application using Vibe Coding! This chapter is where the concepts we've discussed transform into action. We'll walk through the creation of a simple, practical project step-by-step, focusing entirely on the conversational process, your role as the director, and the iterative dance with your AI co-creator.

Remember, the goal here is *not* to learn programming syntax or become a technical expert overnight. The goal is to experience the Vibe Coding workflow firsthand, understand the mindset, and build the confidence to start turning your own ideas into reality. We will deliberately **avoid showing any actual computer code** in this chapter. Our focus will remain squarely on the prompts you give, the hypothetical responses and actions of the AI, and how you observe and refine the results.

Our Project: The "Personal Movie Watchlist"

To make this practical, let's choose a simple, relatable project: a **Personal Movie Watchlist**.

Almost everyone has a list of movies they want to watch, maybe scribbled on a notepad, lost in a notes app, or just floating around in their head. Our goal is to create a very basic web-based tool where we can:

1. Quickly add movie titles we want to watch.
2. See a clear list of these movies.
3. Mark movies as "watched."
4. (Maybe) Remove movies from the list.

It's simple enough to be achievable for a first project, but complex enough to illustrate the key steps of the Vibe Coding process.

The Tool We'll Imagine Using

For this walkthrough, let's imagine we're using an **Integrated Online Platform** like the Replit example discussed in Chapter 4. This type of tool is ideal because it typically combines:

- An AI chat panel (where we'll have our conversation).
- A file explorer (so the AI can create index.html, style.css, script.js files).
- A code editing area (which we'll mostly ignore, letting the AI manage it).
- A preview window or "Run" button (so we can immediately test the results).

Even if you choose to start with a simpler chatbot like ChatGPT, the *conversational process* we outline here remains largely the same; you would just need to handle the testing part separately.

Okay, grab a metaphorical director's chair. Let's begin production on the "Personal Movie Watchlist"!

Step 1: Define the Vibe/Intent (Setting the Creative Direction)

Before we write our first prompt, we need to be clear about what we're building and what we want it to *feel* like. This is like a director setting the vision before shouting "Action!"

- **The Core Problem:** I keep forgetting movies people recommend or trailers I see. My current list is disorganized (or non-existent).
- **The Solution:** A super simple web page where I can quickly type in a movie title and add it to a persistent list. I need to see the list clearly and be able to mark off movies I've watched.
- **The Vibe:** Quick, simple, clean, uncluttered, functional. It doesn't need fancy features right now. I want it to be effortless to add a movie the moment I think of it, and satisfying to mark one as watched. Low friction is key.
- **Core Features (Version 1):**

- o Input field to type a movie title.
- o An "Add Movie" button.
- o A displayed list of added movies.
- o A way to mark each movie as "watched" (maybe a button next to it).
- o (Stretch Goal for V1): A way to remove a movie.
- **Technology (Guidance for the AI):** Let's aim for a standard web application using HTML for structure, CSS for basic styling, and JavaScript for the interactive parts (like adding to the list and marking as watched).

Okay, our directorial brief is set. We know what we want to build and the general feeling we're aiming for. Time to talk to our AI co-creator.

Step 2: Initial Prompting (The First "Action!")

We open our imaginary Replit project, find the AI chat panel, and craft our first instruction. We want to start simple, just getting the basic structure in place. We need to be clear but don't need to over-explain *how* to do it technically.

- **Our First Prompt:**

```
Hi! Please help me create a simple web application called "My
Movie Watchlist".
Use HTML, CSS, and JavaScript.
For the initial structure, I need:
1. A main heading on the page that says "My Movie Watchlist".
2. An input field where I can type a movie title.
3. A button next to the input field that says "Add Movie".
4. An empty area below this where the list of movies will
eventually be displayed.
Please create the basic index.html, style.css, and script.js
files with this structure. Don't worry about making the button
work yet, just set up the visual elements.
```

- **Why this prompt?**
  - o It clearly states the project name and technologies.
  - o It breaks down the required visual elements into a numbered list.
  - o It explicitly tells the AI *not* to worry about functionality yet, keeping the first step simple and focused on structure.
  - o It requests the standard file types for a web project.

We type this into the AI chat panel and hit send. There might be a moment of anticipation. What will the AI come back with?

Step 3: Running & Observing (Reviewing the First Take)

The AI processes our request. After a short pause, it likely responds with something like:

- **Hypothetical AI Response:**

```
Okay, I've created the basic `index.html`, `style.css`, and
`script.js` files for your "My Movie Watchlist" application.
- `index.html` contains the heading, text input field, and the
'Add Movie' button as requested. I've also added a `<div>`
element with an ID like 'movieListArea' to serve as the
container for your movie list later.
- `style.css` is currently empty, as no styling was requested
yet.
- `script.js` is also empty, as the button functionality wasn't
needed for this step.
You can click the 'Run' button to see the basic page structure.
```

Now, it's our turn to act as the tester. We find the "Run" button in our online platform and click it. A preview window likely pops up, showing a very plain webpage.

- **Our Observation:**
  - We see the heading "My Movie Watchlist" at the top. Good.
  - Below it, there's a text box (the input field) and right next to it, a standard, unstyled button labeled "Add Movie". Good.
  - Below that, there's just empty space. We can't *see* the 'movieListArea' div, but we trust the AI created it based on its response.
  - The page looks very basic, no colors or nice fonts yet, but that's expected.
  - We try typing a movie title into the box and clicking the "Add Movie" button. As expected, absolutely nothing happens. The text stays in the box, and the empty area below remains empty.
- **Evaluation:** The AI successfully created the basic visual structure we asked for. It correctly understood the elements needed and deferred the functionality as requested. The first take matches the prompt.

Step 4: Conversational Refinement (Shaping the Scene)

Our basic set is built, but it doesn't *do* anything yet. Time to give our AI co-creator more instructions, refining the scene based on our observations. Our immediate goal is to make the "Add Movie" button actually add the movie title to the list area.

- **Refinement Round 1: Making the Button Work**
  - **Our Prompt:**

```
Thanks, the basic structure looks right. Now, please add the
JavaScript functionality. When the user types a movie title
into the input field and clicks the 'Add Movie' button, I want
the following to happen:
1. The movie title they typed should appear as a new item in
the 'movieListArea' below.
2. The input field should be cleared so they can easily type
another title.
Please modify the `script.js` file to achieve this.
```

  - **Why this prompt?** It clearly describes the *event* (button click), the *condition* (text in input), and the desired *actions* (add to list, clear input) in a step-by-step manner. It also specifies which file likely needs modification.
- **Hypothetical AI Response:**

```
Understood. I've updated the `script.js` file to add an event
listener to the 'Add Movie' button. When clicked, it will:
1. Get the text value from the input field.
2. Create a new list item element (`<li>`) containing that
text.
3. Append this new list item to the 'movieListArea' div.
4. Clear the input field.
Please run the project again to test this functionality.
```

- **Testing Round 1:** We click "Run" again. The page looks the same initially.
  - We type "Inception" into the input field and click "Add Movie".
  - **Observation:** Success! The text "Inception" appears in the area below the button. And the input field is now empty. Great!

- o We try adding another movie. We type "Parasite" and click "Add Movie".
- o **Observation:** "Parasite" appears below "Inception". Excellent! The list is growing.
- o **Evaluation:** The core functionality of adding movies to the list is now working as requested.
- Refinement Round 2: Basic List Styling
  The list works, but it probably looks very plain – just text stacked vertically. Let's add some minimal styling for clarity.
  - o **Our Prompt:**

```
Okay, adding movies works now! Let's add some very basic
styling using CSS.
1. Can you make each movie title in the list appear on its own
line?
2. Add a little bit of spacing (maybe padding or margin) around
each movie title in the list so they aren't jammed together.
3. Remove the default bullet points from the list items.
Please modify the `style.css` file.
```

  - o **Why this prompt?** It targets specific visual improvements and suggests which file to modify. It uses descriptive terms ("own line," "spacing," "remove bullet points") rather than technical CSS properties.
- **Hypothetical AI Response:**

```
Certainly. I've added some basic rules to `style.css` targeting
the list items within 'movieListArea'. I've set them to display
as block elements (which puts them on separate lines), added
some padding around them, and removed the default list-style
bullet points. Run the project to see the updated styling.
```

- **Testing Round 2:** We click "Run". We add a couple of movies ("Dune", "Everything Everywhere All at Once").
  - o **Observation:** The movies now appear neatly stacked, each on its own line, with some visible space between them. The ugly default bullet points are gone. It looks much cleaner.

o **Evaluation:** The basic styling refinement is successful and makes the list much more readable.

We could continue refining the basic adding/displaying functionality, perhaps asking for different fonts, colors, or layout adjustments. But for now, the core mechanism is in place. Let's move on to adding a new feature.

Step 5: Adding Functionality (Introducing a New Scene Element)

Our watchlist lets us add movies, but a key part of the initial "vibe" was being able to mark movies as watched. Let's add that functionality. We need a way to trigger this action for each movie. A simple button next to each title seems appropriate.

- **Adding Functionality Round 1: Adding the "Watched" Button**
  o **Our Prompt:**

```
This is looking good. Now, I need to add a way to mark movies
as watched. Please modify the process so that when a new movie
title is added to the list, a small button appears next to it.
This button should say "Watched?". Don't worry about making the
button functional yet, just make sure it appears next to each
movie title.
```

  o **Why this prompt?** It clearly describes the new element (a button), its text ("Watched?"), and its position (next to each movie title). It also wisely defers the functionality again, breaking the feature down into smaller steps (first appearance, then action).
- **Hypothetical AI Response:**

```
Okay, I've updated the JavaScript code in `script.js`. Now,
when a new movie title is added:
1. It still creates the list item for the title.
2. It *also* creates a button element with the text "Watched?".
3. It appends both the title text and the new button to the
list item, so they appear side-by-side.
Please run and test. The button won't do anything when clicked
yet.
```

- **Testing Round 1:** Click "Run". Add a movie, say "Spirited Away".
  - ○ **Observation:** The title "Spirited Away" appears on the list, and right next to it is a small button labeled "Watched?". Perfect. Add another movie, "The Matrix". It also appears with its own "Watched?" button.
  - ○ **Evaluation:** The AI successfully added the button element visually as requested.
- Adding Functionality Round 2: Making the "Watched" Button Work Now, let's make the button do something. A common way to indicate "watched" is to strike through the text or change its appearance.
  - ○ **Our Prompt:**

Great, the 'Watched?' buttons are appearing. Now, let's add the functionality. When a user clicks the 'Watched?' button next to a movie title, I want the text of that specific movie title to get a line through it (like strikethrough text). Clicking it again should ideally remove the line-through, toggling it back and forth, but just getting the strikethrough to appear on the first click is the main goal for now.

- ○ **Why this prompt?** It specifies the trigger (button click), the target (the specific movie title next to the button), and the desired visual effect (strikethrough). It also suggests a potential toggle behavior but prioritizes the primary action.
- **Hypothetical AI Response:**

Understood. I've added JavaScript code so that when any 'Watched?' button is clicked:
1. It identifies the movie title text element associated with that specific button.
2. It adds a CSS class to that text element (e.g., a class named 'watched-movie').
I've also added a rule to `style.css` for the `.watched-movie` class that applies the `text-decoration: line-through;` style. This should achieve the strikethrough effect when you click the button. I haven't added the toggle functionality yet. Please test it out.

- •
  - **Testing Round 2:** Click "Run". Add "Inception" and "Parasite".
    - o Click the "Watched?" button next to "Inception".
    - o **Observation:** The text "Inception" instantly gets a line drawn through it. Success!
    - o Click the "Watched?" button next to "Parasite".
    - o **Observation:** "Parasite" gets a line through it. "Inception" remains struck through. Good, they work independently.
    - o Click the "Watched?" button next to "Inception" again.
    - o **Observation:** Nothing happens. The line stays. This matches the AI's response (no toggle yet).
    - o **Evaluation:** The core "mark as watched" functionality (visual strikethrough) is working.

We've successfully added a new feature through conversation! We could continue, perhaps adding the toggle functionality or the "Remove" button (our stretch goal), following the same pattern: describe the desired behavior, let the AI generate/modify, test the result, and refine as needed. But let's imagine we encounter a problem.

Step 6: Addressing Errors (Troubleshooting with Your Assistant)

Things don't always go smoothly. AI isn't perfect, and sometimes the code it generates might have bugs, or adding a new feature might unintentionally break something else. Let's simulate a common beginner scenario: the watchlist isn't saving.

- **The Problem:** We've added several movies, marked some as watched. Everything looks great. But then, we accidentally refresh the webpage (or close the browser tab and reopen it).
- **Observation:** Disaster! The watchlist is empty again. All the movies we added are gone. The AI's code only stored the list in the computer's temporary memory for that browser session.

We need to tell the AI about this problem. We don't need to know *why* it happened technically; we just need to describe the *symptom*.

- **Error Reporting Prompt:**

```
Help! I added several movies to my watchlist, and it looked
great. But when I refreshed the webpage, the entire list
disappeared. The movies aren't being saved permanently. How can
I make the list persist even if I close the browser or refresh
the page?
```

-
- **Why this prompt?** It clearly describes the unexpected behavior (list disappears on refresh) and states the desired outcome (list should persist). It asks for a solution without needing technical terms.
- **Hypothetical AI Response (Troubleshooting):**

Ah, that's a common issue! By default, the data added using JavaScript like this only exists while the page is loaded. To make the list persist across sessions, we need to use the browser's **Local Storage**.
Here's the plan:
1. When a movie is added, we'll save the entire list of movies to Local Storage.
2. When a movie is marked as watched, we'll update the list in Local Storage.
3. When the page first loads, we'll check if there's a list saved in Local Storage. If so, we'll load it and display it immediately.
Would you like me to modify the `script.js` file to implement saving and loading using Local Storage?

- **Why this response is helpful:** It diagnoses the problem in simple terms, explains the solution concept (Local Storage), outlines the steps needed, and asks for confirmation before proceeding.
- **Our Follow-up Prompt:**

Yes, please implement saving and loading using Local Storage as you described. That sounds like exactly what I need.

- **Hypothetical AI Response (Implementing Fix):**

Okay, I have updated `script.js`. I've added functions to:
- `saveMoviesToLocalStorage()` which converts the current movie list data into a format suitable for storage and saves it. This function is now called whenever a movie is added or its watched status changes.
- `loadMoviesFromLocalStorage()` which runs when the page loads. It checks for saved data, retrieves it, and rebuilds the

```
movie list display.
Please try running the application again. Add some movies, mark
one as watched, then refresh the page. Your list should now
reappear.
```

- **Testing the Fix:** We click "Run".
    - o Add "Movie A", "Movie B", "Movie C".
    - o Mark "Movie B" as watched (it gets a strikethrough).
    - o Now, the crucial test: Refresh the webpage.
    - o **Observation:** Success! The page reloads, and the list immediately shows "Movie A", "Movie B" (still with a strikethrough), and "Movie C". The data persisted!
    - o **Evaluation:** The AI correctly identified the problem and implemented a working solution based on our description of the symptoms. We didn't need to understand the technical details of Local Storage ourselves.

This error-handling loop – **Observe Problem -> Describe Symptom -> AI Diagnoses/Suggests -> Confirm Fix -> AI Implements -> Test Fix** – is a vital part of the Vibe Coding process. Your role is clear observation and description; the AI's role is diagnosis and implementation.

Step 7: Vibe Check (Aligning with the Feeling)

Our app is now functional! It adds movies, marks them as watched, and saves the list. But does it match the initial "vibe" we defined? Quick, simple, clean, uncluttered, effortless? Let's step back and evaluate the overall feel.

- **Creator's Evaluation:** "Okay, it works, which is amazing. But it still looks very plain. The standard browser font is a bit harsh, the spacing is okay but could be more generous, and the buttons look very basic. It functions, but the 'vibe' isn't quite 'calm and effortless' yet. It feels a bit stark."

Based on this evaluation, we can give the AI more subjective, aesthetic feedback.

- **Vibe Check Prompt:**

```
The functionality is great now, thanks! Let's refine the visual
'vibe' a bit to make it feel calmer and cleaner.
1. Can we change the font for the entire page to something
```

simpler and softer, like Arial or Helvetica?
2. Could you increase the spacing between the movie items in the list a little more?
3. Can we make the "Add Movie" and "Watched?" buttons look a bit nicer? Maybe give them slightly rounded corners and a softer background color instead of the default grey? Perhaps a light blue?
Please update the `style.css` file.

- **Why this prompt?** It uses subjective terms ("calmer," "cleaner," "softer," "nicer") linked to specific visual elements (font, spacing, buttons) and suggests concrete changes (Arial, rounded corners, light blue background).
- **Hypothetical AI Response:**

Certainly. I've updated `style.css` to:
1. Set the default font for the body to Arial, with sans-serif as a fallback.
2. Increased the bottom margin for the list items within 'movieListArea'.
3. Added styles for the buttons, including a light blue background (`lightblue`), white text color, removed the default border, added some padding, and applied a small `border-radius` for rounded corners.
Run the project to see if this aligns better with the desired vibe.

- **Testing the Vibe:** Click "Run". Add some movies.
  - **Observation:** The font is now cleaner and less harsh. The movies in the list have more breathing room. The buttons look much more modern and less jarring with their light blue background and rounded corners.
  - **Evaluation:** This feels much better! The small visual tweaks significantly improved the overall "vibe," making it feel simpler and more pleasant to use, closer to our initial intent.

Step 8: Acceptance (Knowing When Version 1 is Done)

We've built our core features, fixed a major bug (persistence), and tweaked the aesthetics to match our desired vibe. Could we add more? Absolutely. We could add ratings, genres, links to trailers, sorting options, user accounts... the list is endless.

But for Version 1, based on our initial simple goals, this might be a good place to pause and accept what we've built. It solves the core problem (tracking movies to watch) in a simple, clean way that matches our intended vibe.

- **Creator's Decision:** "This is great! It does exactly what I set out to do for the first version. It's simple, it works, it saves my list, and it feels good to use. I'll accept this as Version 1. I have ideas for future improvements, but I can tackle those later using the same Vibe Coding process."

This acceptance step is important. Vibe Coding's iterative nature means you *could* keep tweaking and adding forever. Knowing when a version meets its core goals and is "good enough" for now is a key part of the process. It allows you to celebrate the accomplishment and avoid getting stuck in endless refinement.

Our First Project: Complete!

And there we have it. We just walked through the entire Vibe Coding process, from defining an idea to building a functional, persistent, and aesthetically considered (albeit simple) web application, all through conversational prompts and iterative refinement – **without writing a single line of code ourselves.**

We acted as the Director:

- We defined the **vision** and **vibe**.
- We gave clear **instructions** (prompts).
- We **tested** the results meticulously.
- We provided specific **feedback** for refinement and bug fixing.
- We **added features** incrementally.
- We **evaluated** the final product against our goals.
- We decided when **Version 1** was complete.

The AI acted as our tireless, multi-skilled Crew:

- It **understood** our natural language requests.
- It **generated** the necessary HTML, CSS, and JavaScript.
- It **modified** the code based on our feedback.
- It helped **diagnose** and **fix** errors.
- It implemented both **functional** and **aesthetic** changes.

This walkthrough aimed to demystify the *process* and the *mindset* of Vibe Coding. It's less about knowing the technical answers upfront and more about knowing how to ask the right questions, how to evaluate the results critically, and how to guide your AI partner effectively through conversation.

The "Personal Movie Watchlist" is just one simple example. Think back to the ideas currently residing in your own "Idea Graveyard." Could you use this same process to build a basic version of one of them? A simple portfolio page? A tool to track your freelance projects? A habit tracker?

The power of Vibe Coding lies in its accessibility. It invites you, the creator, the visionary, the non-technical expert, to participate directly in building the digital tools you imagine.

Now that you've seen the process in action, the next step is to learn a bit more about crafting those all-important prompts – the instructions you give to your AI co-creator. Let's explore the art of the prompt in the next chapter.

CHAPTER 6: TALKING TO YOUR AI: THE ART OF THE PROMPT

This Chapter Covers

- **Focus:** Writing effective **prompts** (instructions) is crucial for Vibe Coding.
- **Core Idea:** Clear prompts yield better AI results; it's the key practical skill.
- **Key Prompting Principles:**
    1. **Be Clear & Specific:** Detail your exact needs.
    2. **Break It Down:** Use small, manageable steps.
    3. **Provide Context:** Explain the project goal/state.
    4. **Describe the 'Vibe':** Communicate the desired feel/aesthetics.
    5. **Ask for Changes Precisely:** Specify *what* and *how* to modify.
    6. **Describe Errors Accurately:** Detail symptoms & error messages.
- **Skill Development:** Prompting improves with practice & experimentation.

"The single biggest problem in communication is the illusion that it has taken place."
- George Bernard Shaw

In our journey so far, we've explored the exciting potential of Vibe Coding, met our AI co-creators (the tools), and even walked through building our first simple application, the "Personal Movie Watchlist." You saw how the core process relies on a conversational back-and-forth: you describe, the AI builds, you test, you refine.

Now, we need to zoom in on the most critical part of that conversation: **your instructions**. In the world of AI, these instructions are called **prompts**. Think of prompts as the way you, the Director, communicate your vision to your incredibly powerful, but sometimes very literal, AI Crew.

Why dedicate a whole chapter to this? Because the **quality of your prompts dramatically impacts the quality of the results you get.**

Imagine trying to guide a human assistant. If you mumble vague instructions like "Make it look nice" or "Fix the thingy," you're likely to get confused looks, incorrect results, or wasted effort. The same is true, perhaps even more so, when working with AI. While AI language models are incredibly sophisticated at understanding language, they aren't mind-readers. They can't intuit your exact intentions from ambiguous requests. They thrive on clarity.

Learning to write effective prompts is, therefore, the single most important practical skill you can develop to become successful and efficient at Vibe Coding. It's not about learning code; it's about learning how to **communicate effectively with your AI assistant.** It's less technical wizardry and more the art of clear instruction, thoughtful guidance, and precise language.

Think of it like learning to give good directions. A poorly worded prompt is like telling someone to "go down the street a bit and turn somewhere." A well-crafted prompt is like saying, "Walk three blocks north on Main Street, turn left at the bakery with the green awning, and look for the blue door." One leads to confusion, the other leads to the desired destination.

The good news is that writing effective prompts doesn't require technical genius. It relies on principles that are actually quite intuitive, especially for creative individuals used to articulating ideas. It involves being clear, breaking things down, providing context, describing the desired feeling, asking for changes specifically, and explaining problems accurately.

In this chapter, we'll explore these key principles in detail. We'll provide practical, actionable tips specifically for non-technical creators, illustrated with plenty of examples showing the difference between weak prompts that lead to frustration and strong prompts that lead to success. Mastering this "art of the prompt" is your key to truly unlocking the creative power of Vibe Coding.

Principle 1: Be Clear and Specific (Say Exactly What You Mean)

This is the absolute foundation of effective prompting. Vagueness is the enemy of good AI output. When your instructions are unclear or ambiguous, the AI is forced to make assumptions. Sometimes it might guess correctly, but often it will produce something generic, incomplete, or simply wrong.

- **Why Vagueness Fails:** An AI doesn't have your personal context, aesthetic taste, or deep understanding of your project's goals unless you provide it. A vague prompt like "Make a website section" could result in almost anything – a block of text, an image gallery, a contact form? The AI has no way to know what you *really* want. It will likely generate the most common or generic interpretation, which might be far from your actual vision.
- **The Power of Specificity:** When you are clear and specific, you leave less room for misinterpretation. You guide the AI directly towards the desired outcome. This involves:

- o Using precise nouns and verbs.
- o Defining terms if they might be ambiguous.
- o Specifying quantities, dimensions, colors, text content, etc.
- o Stating constraints or requirements clearly.

Let's look at some examples comparing weak, vague prompts with strong, specific ones:

Example Scenario 1: Creating a Button

- • **Weak Prompt:** "Add a button."
  - o *Potential AI Output:* The AI might generate a default, unstyled HTML button with generic text like "Button" or no text at all. It has no idea what the button is for or how it should look.
  - o *Result:* You get *a* button, but it's probably useless and needs immediate refinement.
- • **Strong Prompt:** "Please create an HTML button for my webpage.
  - o The text displayed on the button should be 'Download Brochure'.
  - o Give the button a unique ID attribute: id='brochure-download-btn'.
  - o Add a CSS class attribute: class='cta-button'.
    We will style the 'cta-button' class later using CSS."
  - o *Potential AI Output:* The AI generates the specific HTML: <button id='brochure-download-btn' class='cta-button'>Download Brochure</button>.
  - o *Result:* You get exactly the button element you need, clearly labeled and ready for styling and functionality later. Much more efficient!

Example Scenario 2: Requesting a Layout

- • **Weak Prompt:** "Make a layout for my homepage."
  - o *Potential AI Output:* The AI might generate a very generic layout – maybe a header, a single column of text, and a footer. Or it might ask you for more details, forcing another prompt cycle.
  - o *Result:* Unlikely to match your vision; too much guesswork involved for the AI.
- • **Strong Prompt:** "Create a basic two-column layout for the main content area of my homepage using HTML and CSS.
  - o The left column should take up about 30% of the width and contain a navigation menu (we'll add the menu items later, just create a placeholder div with id='left-nav').

- o The right column should take up the remaining 70% of the width and be the main content area (create a placeholder div with id='main-content').
- o Ensure there's a small gap or margin between the two columns for visual separation."
- o *Potential AI Output:* The AI generates the necessary HTML structure (e.g., using divs) and the corresponding CSS (e.g., using Flexbox or Grid) to create the specified two-column layout with the given proportions and IDs.
- o *Result:* You get the specific layout structure you requested, ready for you to populate with content or further instructions.

Example Scenario 3: Simple Calculation Logic

- • **Weak Prompt:** "Calculate the total."
  - o *Potential AI Output:* The AI has no idea *what* total to calculate. It might ask for clarification or make a completely wrong guess based on previous conversation context (if any).
  - o *Result:* Failure or incorrect output.
- • **Strong Prompt:** "Please write a JavaScript function named calculateOrderTotal.
  - o It should accept two arguments: itemPrice and quantity.
  - o Inside the function, it should multiply itemPrice by quantity.
  - o It should then return the result of this multiplication."
  - o *Potential AI Output:* The AI generates the specific JavaScript function:

```
function calculateOrderTotal(itemPrice, quantity) {
  return itemPrice * quantity;
}
```

- o (Remember: we're not showing code in the final chapter, but this illustrates the *specificity* the AI can handle).
- o *Result:* You get the precise piece of logic you needed, clearly defined.

Tips for Being Clear and Specific:

- • **Use Action Verbs:** Start prompts with clear verbs like "Create," "Add," "Change," "Remove," "Write," "Generate," "Explain," "Modify."

- **Identify Elements Precisely:** Refer to specific elements using their text, ID, class, or position (e.g., "the button labeled 'Submit'," "the image in the header," "the second paragraph in the 'About Us' section").
- **Specify Attributes and Content:** Clearly state required text content, ID names, class names, image URLs, colors (use specific names like red, lightblue, or hex codes like #FF0000 if you know them), font names, etc.
- **Quantify When Possible:** Instead of "make it bigger," try "increase the font size by 2 pixels" or "make the image width 300 pixels."
- **Define Constraints:** If there are rules or limitations, state them. "Ensure the total width does not exceed 800 pixels." "Use only standard HTML tags, no custom elements."
- **Review Your Prompt:** Before hitting send, reread your prompt. Is it unambiguous? Could it be interpreted in multiple ways? If so, refine it.

Being clear and specific might feel like a bit more effort upfront, but it saves enormous amounts of time and frustration in the long run by minimizing misunderstandings and ensuring the AI delivers results closer to your actual intent on the first try.

Principle 2: Break It Down (Think Small Steps, Not Giant Leaps)

When you have a big idea for an app or website, it's tempting to try and describe the whole thing to the AI in one go. "Build me a social media platform for cat lovers with profiles, photo uploads, commenting, and direct messaging!" While the AI might *attempt* such a request, the results are likely to be messy, incomplete, buggy, and overwhelming for you to test and refine.

Just like you wouldn't try to build a house by telling the crew "Build a house!" and walking away, you shouldn't try to vibe code complex projects in one giant leap. The key is to **break down your big vision into smaller, manageable steps or features.**

- **Why Giant Prompts Fail:**
    - **Increased Complexity for AI:** Handling numerous interconnected requirements simultaneously increases the chance of the AI making errors, forgetting details, or creating conflicting code.
    - **Difficult Testing:** If the AI generates a huge amount of code for multiple features at once, how do you test it effectively? If something is broken, it's much harder to pinpoint where the problem lies.

- o **Overwhelming Output:** The AI might respond with pages and pages of code, which can be intimidating and difficult to assess, even if you're not reading it in detail.
  - o **Loss of Iterative Control:** You lose the benefit of the rapid feedback loop. You can't easily test and refine one small piece before moving to the next.
- **The Power of Small Steps:** Approaching your project incrementally, focusing on one feature or refinement at a time, mirrors good practice in traditional software development and works exceptionally well with Vibe Coding.
  - o **Easier for the AI:** Simpler, focused prompts are easier for the AI to understand and execute correctly.
  - o **Targeted Testing:** You can test each small piece as it's built, ensuring it works before adding more complexity.
  - o **Manageable Output:** The AI responds with smaller, more focused code changes or additions.
  - o **Faster Feedback Loop:** You get results quickly for each step, allowing for rapid refinement and maintaining momentum.
  - o **Simpler Debugging:** If an error occurs after adding one small feature, you know exactly where to focus your troubleshooting prompts.

Let's revisit our "Personal Movie Watchlist" from Chapter 5. We didn't ask the AI to build the whole thing at once. We broke it down:

1. **Prompt:** Create the basic HTML structure (heading, input, button, list area). -> **Test:** Structure appears.
2. **Prompt:** Make the "Add Movie" button add items to the list and clear the input. -> **Test:** Adding works.
3. **Prompt:** Add basic CSS styling to the list. -> **Test:** List looks cleaner.
4. **Prompt:** Add a "Watched?" button next to each item (visual only). -> **Test:** Buttons appear.
5. **Prompt:** Make the "Watched?" button apply strikethrough style on click. -> **Test:** Marking as watched works.
6. **Prompt:** Fix the issue where the list disappears on refresh (implement persistence). -> **Test:** Persistence works.
7. **Prompt:** Refine the visual "vibe" (fonts, spacing, button styles). -> **Test:** Looks better.

Each step built upon the previous one, allowing us to test and confirm functionality along the way.

Example Scenario: Building a Simple Blog

- **Complex Request (Likely to Fail or Be Messy):** "Build me a simple blog website. It needs a homepage showing recent posts, individual pages for each post, a way for me to write new posts, and a basic contact form. Use a clean design."
- **Broken Down Steps (Much Better):**
    1. **Prompt 1:** "Set up the basic HTML and CSS for a blog homepage. Include a header with the blog title 'My Creative Journey', a main area for post summaries (use placeholder text for now), and a simple footer." -> **Test:** Basic layout appears.
    2. **Prompt 2:** "Create the HTML structure for how a single blog post summary should look on the homepage. Include a placeholder for a post title, a short excerpt, and a 'Read More' link." -> **Test:** Placeholder summary structure looks right.
    3. **Prompt 3:** "Now, create the HTML structure for the individual blog post page. It needs a large area for the post title, another for the main post content, and maybe a section for comments below (just a placeholder heading for now)." -> **Test:** Single post page structure looks okay.
    4. **Prompt 4:** "Let's add some basic navigation. In the header on both the homepage and single post page, add links for 'Home' and 'About'." -> **Test:** Navigation appears.
    5. **Prompt 5:** "Now, think about the 'Write New Post' functionality. What would be a simple way to implement that without needing a complex backend database for now?" (Asking for suggestions first). -> **AI Responds with options.**
    6. **Prompt 6 (Based on AI suggestion):** "Okay, let's try the simple approach first. Can you create a separate password-protected HTML page called admin.html with a form where I can enter a post title and the main post content (using a large text area)?" -> **Test:** Admin page structure appears.
    7. ...and so on, tackling saving/displaying posts, the contact form, and styling incrementally.

Tips for Breaking It Down:

- **Think Functionally:** What is the smallest piece of functionality you can build and test first? (e.g., just displaying something, making one button work).
- **Separate Structure, Functionality, and Style:** Often, it's effective to prompt for the basic HTML structure first, then add the JavaScript functionality, and finally refine the CSS styling.
- **Build Incrementally:** Get one feature working reasonably well before moving on to the next.

- **Use Placeholders:** Don't try to get all the final text or images perfect in the first go. Use placeholder text ("Lorem ipsum...") or simple placeholder divs that you can populate or style later.
- **Test After Each Step:** This is crucial. Run the code after each significant prompt to ensure the change worked as expected and didn't break anything else.

Breaking down your project into small, logical steps is fundamental to managing the Vibe Coding process effectively. It keeps the interactions manageable, makes testing easier, and allows you to build momentum and confidence as you see each piece fall into place.

Principle 3: Provide Context (Help the AI Understand the Big Picture)

Imagine asking someone "How do I get there?" without telling them where "there" is or where you are starting from. They can't possibly give you useful directions! Similarly, AI assistants work much better when they have some context about your project and your request.

While you break down tasks into small steps, it's often helpful to remind the AI (or provide initial context) about the overall goal. Without context, the AI might make assumptions or generate code that doesn't quite fit the larger picture.

- **Why Context Matters:**
  - **Better Assumptions:** Knowing the overall purpose helps the AI make more relevant assumptions when your prompt isn't perfectly specific.
  - **Appropriate Choices:** Context guides the AI in choosing appropriate technologies, code structures, or even tone (e.g., code for a children's game vs. a financial tool).
  - **Consistency:** Reminding the AI of the project context helps maintain consistency across different features or sections.
  - **Efficiency:** Reduces the need for the AI to ask clarifying questions.
- **Types of Context to Provide:**
  - **Overall Project Goal:** Briefly state what you are building. ("I'm creating a portfolio website to showcase my photography.")
  - **Target Audience:** Who is this app/website for? ("This is an educational game for preschoolers.")
  - **Current State/Previous Steps:** Remind the AI what has already been built or decided. ("We already created the HTML form; now I need the JavaScript validation for the email field.")

- o **Technology Stack (If Known/Relevant):** Mention the core technologies being used. ("Remember we are using HTML, CSS, and vanilla JavaScript for this project.")
- o **Specific Files (If Applicable):** If working in an environment like Replit, refer to specific filenames. ("Please add the following CSS rules to the style.css file.")

Let's see how context makes a difference:

Example Scenario 1: Generating a List

- **No Context Prompt:** "Generate code for a list."
  - o *Potential AI Output:* The AI might generate a simple HTML unordered list (<ul><li>Item 1</li>...</ul>) or maybe a Python list my_list = []. It has no idea what kind of list or where it fits.
  - o *Result:* Likely not what you needed, or requires significant modification.
- **With Context Prompt:** "I'm building a recipe website using HTML. On the recipe page (recipe.html), below the heading with the recipe name, I need to display the ingredients. Please generate the HTML code for an unordered list (<ul>) to display the ingredients. Use a CSS class class='ingredient-list' for the <ul> tag. For now, just include placeholder list items like 'Ingredient 1', 'Ingredient 2'."
  - o *Potential AI Output:* The AI generates the specific HTML structure within the context of a recipe page:

```
<ul class='ingredient-list'>
  <li>Ingredient 1</li>
  <li>Ingredient 2</li>
</ul>
```

- o *Result:* You get the correctly structured list, ready to be populated with actual ingredients later, and styled using the specified class.

Example Scenario 2: Requesting Button Styling

- **No Context Prompt:** "Make the button look nicer."

- o *Potential AI Output:* The AI might apply some generic "nice" styles (maybe padding, a default color), but it might not match the existing design or the intended feel of the application.
- o *Result:* Hit or miss. Might require immediate refinement.
- **With Context Prompt:** "For the 'My Movie Watchlist' web app we are building, I want to improve the styling of the 'Add Movie' button (id='add-movie-btn') and the 'Watched?' buttons (which have the class class='watched-btn', let's assume we added that class). The overall vibe is clean and simple. Please update style.css to:
  - o Give both types of buttons a light grey background.
  - o Set the text color to dark grey.
  - o Add slightly rounded corners.
  - o Ensure there's a little padding inside the buttons."
  - o *Potential AI Output:* The AI updates the style.css file with rules targeting the specific button ID and class, applying the requested styles (background, color, border-radius, padding) consistent with the "clean and simple" vibe.
  - o *Result:* The buttons are styled appropriately within the context of the existing project and desired aesthetic.

Tips for Providing Context:

- **Start with the Big Picture:** In your very first prompt for a new project, briefly explain what you're building.
- **Refer Back:** In subsequent prompts, especially when starting a new feature, briefly remind the AI of the context if needed (e.g., "Continuing with the bakery website...").
- **Mention Specific Elements/Files:** When asking for changes, refer to the specific IDs, classes, or filenames involved.
- **State Your Goal:** Sometimes explaining *why* you need something helps the AI provide a better solution. ("I need to add error handling here *because* users might enter text instead of numbers.")
- **Don't Overdo It:** You don't need to repeat the entire project history in every prompt. Just provide enough context for the current request to make sense. The AI usually maintains context within a single session (though remember the "context window" limits mentioned in Chapter 4).

Providing context is like giving your AI co-creator a map and a compass along with your specific instructions. It helps ensure the pieces it builds fit together correctly and align with your overall destination.

Principle 4: Describe the 'Vibe' (Communicate the Feeling)

This principle is closely related to providing context but focuses specifically on the **aesthetic, emotional, and experiential qualities** you want your creation to have. Remember, Vibe Coding isn't just about function; it's also about the *feel*. And surprisingly, modern AI models can often interpret and act upon instructions related to these more subjective qualities.

- **Why Describe the Vibe?**
  - **Guides Aesthetic Choices:** Telling the AI the desired vibe (e.g., "playful," "professional," "calm," "energetic") helps it make more appropriate choices regarding colors, fonts, layout density, imagery suggestions, and even the tone of any generated text.
  - **Ensures User Experience Alignment:** It helps ensure the final product feels right for the intended audience and purpose. A meditation app should feel calming; a children's game should feel fun.
  - **Leverages Your Creative Strengths:** As a non-technical creator, your intuition about aesthetics and user experience is a major asset. Describing the vibe allows you to leverage this strength directly in the development process.
  - **More Engaging Interaction:** It makes the process feel more creative and less purely mechanical.
- **How to Describe the Vibe:**
  - **Use Adjectives:** Employ descriptive words: "clean," "minimalist," "bold," "elegant," "retro," "futuristic," "friendly," "corporate," "whimsical," "serious," "inviting," "exclusive."
  - **Reference Analogies/Metaphors:** "Make it feel like a cozy library." "The design should be sharp and precise, like an architect's drawing." "Aim for the energy of a bustling marketplace."
  - **Specify Target Emotion:** "The user should feel reassured after submitting this form." "This section should evoke a sense of wonder."
  - **Combine with Functional Requests:** Integrate vibe descriptions into your specific instructions.

Let's look at how describing the vibe can influence the outcome:

Example Scenario 1: Website Homepage Design

- **Function-Only Prompt:** "Create an HTML homepage with a header, a main content area, and a footer."
  - *Potential AI Output:* A structurally correct but visually bland page with default styles.
- **Vibe-Infused Prompt:** "Create an HTML homepage for a luxury travel agency. The vibe should be **elegant, sophisticated, and inspiring**, evoking a sense of wanderlust. Include a large, impactful

header (perhaps for a stunning photo later), a main content area, and a simple footer. Use placeholder text for now, but keep the structure clean and spacious. Suggest a suitable elegant font family in the CSS."

- *Potential AI Output:* The AI might generate the HTML structure but also add CSS rules that suggest:
  - A spacious layout with generous white space.
  - Placeholders for large imagery.
  - A recommendation for a serif font family (like Times New Roman, Garamond) often associated with elegance.
  - Perhaps even basic color suggestions (e.g., deep blues, golds, or muted tones).
- *Result:* The initial output is already closer to the desired aesthetic feel, providing a better starting point for visual refinement.

Example Scenario 2: App Confirmation Message

- **Function-Only Prompt:** "After the user submits the form, show a message that says 'Data saved'."
  - *Potential AI Output:* Simple text appears: "Data saved". Functional, but dry.
- **Vibe-Infused Prompt:** "After the user submits the contact form on my 'Happy Paws Pet Sitting' website, show a confirmation message. The vibe should be **friendly, warm, and reassuring**. Can you suggest some text for the message and make it appear in a visually soft, perhaps light green, notification box?"
  - *Potential AI Output:* The AI might suggest text like: "Got it! Thanks for reaching out. We'll be in touch soon! 🐾" and provide the HTML/CSS/JS to display this message in a styled box (e.g., light green background, rounded corners).
  - *Result:* The confirmation feels more integrated with the brand's personality and provides a better user experience.

Tips for Describing the Vibe:

- **Create a Vibe Palette:** Before you start, jot down a few keywords that describe the desired look and feel.
- **Use Sensory Language:** Think about how you want the user to *feel*.
- **Be Consistent:** Try to maintain a consistent vibe throughout your application unless you intentionally want different sections to feel distinct.
- **Combine with Specifics:** Vibe descriptions work best when paired with concrete instructions. "Make the button **bold and attention-**

grabbing (vibe) by giving it a bright red background and white text (specifics)."

- **Iterate on the Vibe:** Just like functionality, the vibe might need refinement. If the AI's interpretation isn't quite right, provide more specific aesthetic feedback in the next prompt. ("That blue is too bright; try a softer, more muted blue.")

Don't be afraid to inject personality and feeling into your prompts. Your AI co-creator can often respond to these cues, helping you build applications that not only work well but also resonate emotionally and aesthetically with your users.

Principle 5: How to Ask for Changes (The Art of Revision)

Much of Vibe Coding involves refining what the AI has already generated. Perhaps the layout isn't quite right, a button needs different text, or you want to add an element you forgot initially. Knowing how to clearly ask for specific modifications is essential for efficient iteration.

- **Why Clear Revision Prompts Matter:** Ambiguous requests for changes can lead the AI to modify the wrong element, misunderstand the desired alteration, or even break existing functionality. Specificity is just as important when revising as it is during initial creation.
- **Common Revision Scenarios & Prompt Patterns:**
  - **Changing Text Content:**
    - *Goal:* Change the main heading.
    - *Weak Prompt:* "Change the title." (Which title? To what?)
    - *Strong Prompt:* "Change the text inside the <h1> heading at the top of index.html from 'My Movie Watchlist' to 'My Ultimate Film Log'."
  - **Modifying Styles (CSS):**
    - *Goal:* Make paragraph text larger.
    - *Weak Prompt:* "Bigger text." (Which text? How much bigger?)
    - *Strong Prompt:* "In the style.css file, find the rule for paragraph tags (p). Increase the font-size property to 18px." (Or, more conversationally: "Make the regular paragraph text slightly larger, maybe around 18 pixels.")
  - **Adding New Elements:**
    - *Goal:* Add an image below the header.
    - *Weak Prompt:* "Put an image here." (Where exactly? Which image?)
    - *Strong Prompt:* "In index.html, immediately after the closing </header> tag, please insert an <img> tag. Set its

src attribute to 'images/logo.png' and give it an alt attribute that says 'My Website Logo'."

- o **Removing Elements:**
  - ▪ *Goal:* Get rid of a section.
  - ▪ *Weak Prompt:* "Delete that section." (Which one?)
  - ▪ *Strong Prompt:* "Please remove the entire <div> element that has the ID promo-banner from the index.html file, including all the content inside it."
- o **Rearranging Elements:**
  - ▪ *Goal:* Move a button.
  - ▪ *Weak Prompt:* "Move the button." (Which button? Where to?)
  - ▪ *Strong Prompt:* "In the footer section of index.html, move the 'Privacy Policy' link so that it appears *before* the 'Terms of Service' link."
- o **Changing Element Attributes:**
  - ▪ *Goal:* Make a link open in a new tab.
  - ▪ *Weak Prompt:* "New tab link." (Which link?)
  - ▪ *Strong Prompt:* "Find the link (<a> tag) for 'External Site' in the main content area. Add the attribute target='_blank' to it so it opens in a new browser tab when clicked."

Tips for Asking for Changes:

- • ***Be Specific About What to Change:*** Identify the element clearly (by ID, class, tag type, text content, or position).
- • ***Be Specific About How to Change It:*** State the desired new text, style value, attribute, or position.
- • **Refer to Files if Necessary:** If working with multiple files, specify which one needs modification (index.html, style.css, script.js).
- • **One Major Change Per Prompt:** While you can sometimes bundle small, related changes, it's generally safer to request one significant modification at a time, then test the result before asking for the next change. This makes troubleshooting easier if something breaks.
- • **Confirm Understanding:** If the change is complex, you might ask the AI to explain how it plans to implement it before it generates the code.

Think of revisions like giving notes to your AI apprentice after they've shown you their work. Clear, specific feedback leads to faster, more accurate corrections.

Principle 6: How to Describe Errors (Effective Troubleshooting)

As we saw in Chapter 5, things will inevitably go wrong sometimes. The AI might generate buggy code, or a change you requested might have unintended consequences. Your ability to clearly describe the problem is crucial for getting effective help from your AI assistant. Remember, you don't need to know *why* the error is happening, just *what* is happening.

- **Why Clear Error Descriptions Matter:** If you just say "It's broken," the AI has almost no information to work with. Describing the specific symptoms helps the AI narrow down the potential causes and suggest relevant solutions.
- **Effective Ways to Describe Errors:**
  - **Describe the Unexpected Behavior:** State exactly what you observed happening versus what you expected.
    - *Weak Prompt:* "The list isn't working right."
    - *Strong Prompt:* "When I add a movie title with an apostrophe in it, like 'Schindler's List', it adds it to the list okay, but then the 'Watched?' button next to it doesn't work. Buttons for movies without apostrophes work fine." (This gives the AI a huge clue about where the problem might lie).
    - *Another Strong Prompt:* "After I added the 'Remove' button feature, marking movies as watched stopped working entirely. Clicking the 'Watched?' button does nothing now." (This provides context about when the error started).
  - **Quote Error Messages:** If you see specific error messages in your browser's console or the testing environment, copy and paste them exactly into your prompt. These messages often contain precise technical clues that the AI can interpret.
    - *Weak Prompt:* "I got a JavaScript error."
    - *Strong Prompt:* "When I click the 'Add Movie' button, nothing happens, and I see this error message in the browser console: Uncaught TypeError: document.getElementById(...) is null in script.js:15. What does this mean and how can I fix line 15 in script.js?"
  - **Explain Failed Goals:** If you asked the AI to do something and it didn't work as expected, explain the discrepancy.
    - *Weak Prompt:* "The styling is wrong."
    - *Strong Prompt:* "I asked you to make the background color light blue, but when I run the code, the background is still white. Can you please check the CSS rule you added to style.css?"
  - **Provide Steps to Reproduce (If Possible):** If the error only happens under specific conditions, describe those steps.
    - *Strong Prompt:* "There's a bug: 1. Add three movies. 2. Mark the second movie as watched. 3. Refresh the

page. 4. Expected: The list reloads with the second movie marked. Actual: The list reloads, but *none* of the movies are marked as watched anymore."

Tips for Describing Errors:

- **Be Specific About Symptoms:** What did you see? What did you hear (if applicable)? What happened versus what should have happened?
- **Include Error Messages:** Copy and paste them verbatim if you see any.
- **Provide Context:** When did the error start? What were you doing just before it happened? Did it occur after a specific change request?
- **Isolate the Problem (If Possible):** If you can identify which specific action triggers the error, mention it.
- **Stay Calm:** Frustration is normal, but clear, objective descriptions are more helpful to the AI than emotional outbursts.

Treat your AI assistant like a helpful (but non-psychic) technical support agent. Give it the clear, specific details of the problem, and it stands a much better chance of helping you find the solution.

Putting It All Together: Prompting as a Skill

Writing effective prompts is the core practical skill of Vibe Coding. It's how you translate your vision into instructions the AI can understand and act upon. It's how you guide the iterative process of refinement and troubleshooting.

Let's summarize the key principles:

1. **Be Clear and Specific:** Avoid ambiguity. State exactly what you need.
2. **Break It Down:** Tackle complex projects in small, manageable steps.
3. **Provide Context:** Help the AI understand the bigger picture and purpose.
4. **Describe the 'Vibe':** Communicate the desired look, feel, and user experience.
5. **Ask for Changes Precisely:** Clearly identify what needs modification and how.
6. **Describe Errors Accurately:** Focus on symptoms and provide specific details.

Like any skill, effective prompting improves with **practice**. Don't expect your first prompts to be perfect. You'll learn through trial and error. You'll see how the AI responds to different phrasing. You'll discover what kinds of instructions work best with the specific tools you use.

A Mini-Scenario Integrating Multiple Tips:

Imagine you're working on the homepage for your bakery website ("Bea's Bakery"). You've already got a header.

- **Your Goal:** Add a section showcasing three featured pastries with images and short descriptions, making it look warm and inviting.
- **Potential Prompt Sequence:**
    1. **(Break Down & Context):** "Continuing with the 'Bea's Bakery' homepage (index.html), below the main header section, I want to add a new section to feature three popular pastries. Please create a <div> for this section with id='featured-pastries'." (AI creates the basic container div).
    2. **(Break Down & Specifics):** "Inside the featured-pastries div, I need structure for three items displayed side-by-side (maybe using columns or flexbox in CSS later). For each item, include:
        - A placeholder for an image (<img> tag).
        - A placeholder for the pastry name (<h3> tag).
        - A placeholder for a short description (<p> tag)." (AI generates the HTML structure for three items).
    3. **(Adding Content & Specifics):** "Okay, let's populate the first featured item.
        - Set the src of the first <img> tag to 'images/croissant.jpg' and the alt text to 'Flaky Butter Croissant'.
        - Change the first <h3> text to 'Butter Croissant'.
        - Change the first <p> text to 'Our best-selling classic, layers of flaky, buttery goodness.'" (AI updates the first item).
        - *(Repeat for items 2 and 3).*
    4. **(Vibe & Style):** "Now let's style this section in style.css to make it look **warm and inviting**.
        - Make the featured-pastries section have a slightly off-white or cream background color.
        - Use a warm, perhaps slightly rustic-looking font for the pastry names (<h3> tags inside this section). Can you suggest one?
        - Ensure there's good spacing between the three featured items.
        - Make the images responsive so they resize nicely." (AI adds CSS, potentially suggests a font like 'Georgia' or a Google Font, and adds responsive image styles).
    5. **(Testing & Error Description - Hypothetical):** "I ran the code. The layout looks okay, but the images are huge and overlapping! They aren't resizing properly. Can you check the

responsive image styles you added for the <img> tags inside id='featured-pastries'?" (AI revisits and potentially fixes the CSS).

This sequence demonstrates breaking down the task, being specific, providing context, describing the vibe, adding content, and troubleshooting – all through prompting.

Don't Be Afraid to Experiment!

The most important takeaway from this chapter is to view prompting as an interactive skill to be developed.

- Try different ways of phrasing things.
- See how the AI reacts to varying levels of detail.
- Experiment with describing the "vibe."
- Practice breaking down your ideas into smaller steps.
- Don't hesitate to ask the AI clarifying questions ("What do you mean by that?", "Can you explain the code you just gave me?").

The more you practice communicating with your AI co-creator, the better you'll become at translating your vision into effective prompts, and the faster and more satisfying your Vibe Coding journey will be. Clear communication is your superpower in this new world of creation.

CHAPTER 7: COOL THINGS YOU CAN BUILD (AND WHAT MIGHT BE TRICKY)

This Chapter Covers

- **Focus:** Discusses good project types ("Sweet Spot") & limitations for Vibe Coding.
- **Sweet Spot (Good Fits):** Personal sites/portfolios, landing pages, simple e-com fronts (use 3rd-party payments), custom utilities, basic games/automation.
- **Vibe-Friendly Factors:** Clear goal, manageable scope (start small), uses standard features.
- **Limitations (Challenging/Risky):** High complexity, high security (**never** build payment/sensitive data handling; use 3rd parties!), high reliability/performance, very novel features, long-term maintainability.
- **Key Takeaway:** Choose projects suited to Vibe Coding strengths, start simple, understand limits (especially security).

"Wisely, and slow. They stumble that run fast."

- William Shakespeare

You've journeyed through the core concepts of Vibe Coding, met your potential AI co-creators, witnessed a project come to life through conversation, and learned the crucial art of crafting effective prompts. The foundational pieces are in place. Now, perhaps the most exciting question arises: ***What can I actually build with this?***

The answer is both thrilling and nuanced. Vibe Coding, fueled by increasingly powerful AI, throws open doors to digital creation that were previously locked for many non-technical individuals. It allows you to move ideas from your "Idea Graveyard" into tangible reality with unprecedented speed and accessibility. The potential is immense.

However, like any powerful tool, it has areas where it excels and areas where it's less suited, or even potentially risky if used inappropriately. Understanding this landscape – knowing where Vibe Coding shines and where its boundaries currently lie – is key to choosing your projects wisely, setting realistic expectations, and ultimately having a successful and rewarding creative experience.

This chapter is your exploration guide. We'll first dive into the "sweet spot" – showcasing inspiring examples of the kinds of projects that are often well-suited for Vibe Coding, especially for creators without a traditional programming background. Then, we'll constructively and carefully explore the types of projects where Vibe Coding might be challenging or require significant caution. This isn't about limiting your ambition, but about empowering you to make informed choices and use this revolutionary tool effectively.

The Vibe Coding Sweet Spot: Where Your Ideas Can Take Flight

Imagine having a versatile, incredibly fast digital assistant ready to help you build. What kinds of things are particularly well-suited for this partnership? Generally, projects that have a **clear goal**, a **manageable scope** (especially for initial versions), and rely on relatively **standard features and interactions** fall into the Vibe Coding sweet spot. Let's explore some exciting possibilities:

1. Personal Websites & Portfolios:

- **The Dream:** Finally having a professional, beautiful online space to showcase your work, share your story, or build your personal brand. Whether you're an artist, writer, photographer, musician, consultant, or freelancer, a personal website is often essential.
- **Vibe Coding Power:** Building these often involves standard elements that AI excels at generating:
  - **Layouts:** Describe the structure you want (e.g., header with your name/logo, navigation menu, main content area, footer). Ask for specific layouts like single-column, two-column, or grid-based sections.
  - **Image Galleries:** Prompt the AI to create galleries to display your visual work. Ask for different styles (e.g., grid layout, slideshow, lightbox effect where clicking an image enlarges it).
  - **Text Content:** Structure pages like "About Me," "Services," "Portfolio," "Blog," or "Contact." The AI can generate the basic HTML structure for headings, paragraphs, and lists.
  - **Contact Forms:** Ask the AI to create a standard contact form (fields for name, email, message, submit button). *Note:* Handling the *submission* securely often requires extra steps or integration with third-party services, which the AI might be able to help configure.
  - **Basic Styling:** Use "vibe" prompts ("make it minimalist and clean," "give it a creative and colorful feel") combined with

specific requests ("use this font," "make the background this color") to get the look you want.

- **Example Vibe Coding Scenario:** An artist could prompt: "Create a portfolio website. I need a homepage with a grid of my recent paintings. Each painting should link to a separate page showing a larger image and a description. Also include an 'About the Artist' page and a simple contact form. The vibe should be clean, modern, and focus attention on the artwork." The AI could generate the HTML structure, basic CSS, and potentially the JavaScript for gallery interactions.

2. Landing Pages for Ideas & Projects:

- **The Dream:** You have a new business idea, a book concept, a potential course, or a community project, and you want to gauge interest, collect email signups, or present the core concept quickly and professionally without building a full website yet.
- **Vibe Coding Power:** Landing pages are typically single-page sites focused on a specific goal, making them ideal for rapid creation:
  - **Clear Structure:** Prompt for a headline, a compelling description, key benefit bullet points, maybe a spot for an image or video, and a clear call-to-action (CTA).
  - **Signup Forms:** Easily generate forms to collect email addresses (again, integrating with an email marketing service like Mailchimp or ConvertKit for actually *managing* the list is usually a separate step the AI might assist with).
  - **Concise Design:** Focus the AI on creating a clean, persuasive design that directs attention to the CTA. Use vibe prompts like "make it look trustworthy and professional" or "create a sense of urgency."
- **Example Vibe Coding Scenario:** An author could prompt: "Create a landing page for my upcoming sci-fi novel. Include the book title prominently, a compelling tagline, a short synopsis paragraph, a placeholder for the book cover image, and an email signup form with a button saying 'Get Notified on Launch!'. The vibe should be futuristic and intriguing."

3. Simple E-commerce Storefronts (with Integration):

- **The Dream:** Selling your physical products (crafts, art prints, merchandise) or digital products (e-books, templates, music) online without the complexity or cost of a massive e-commerce platform.
- **Vibe Coding Power (with a Caveat):** Vibe Coding is excellent for creating the **storefront** – the part customers see. However, handling secure payments, shopping carts, and order management directly is highly complex and security-critical. The smart approach here is to:

- o **Build the Front-End:** Use Vibe Coding to create attractive product listing pages, individual product detail pages (with descriptions, images, prices), and category pages. Prompt the AI for layouts, image galleries, and text structure.
- o **Integrate with Third-Party Services:** For the actual "buy" button, cart, and checkout, integrate with established, secure platforms. Examples include:
    - **Payment Links/Buttons:** Services like Stripe Checkout, PayPal Buttons, or Gumroad allow you to create simple "Buy Now" buttons or links that handle the entire secure payment process. You can prompt the AI to help you embed the code snippet provided by these services onto your product pages.
    - **Simple E-commerce Widgets:** Platforms like Shopify offer "Lite" plans or Buy Buttons that can be embedded onto any website, providing cart functionality and secure checkout without needing a full Shopify store.
- **Example Vibe Coding Scenario:** A ceramic artist could prompt: "Create a product page for my 'Ocean Glaze Mug'. Include a large image gallery section, a title 'Ocean Glaze Mug', a paragraph description, the price '$45', and dimensions. Below this, add a section where I can later embed a 'Buy Now' button code from my payment processor. The vibe should be earthy, handmade, and high-quality." The AI generates the page structure; the artist then gets the button code from Stripe/PayPal/etc. and prompts the AI: "Add this button code snippet below the product description."

4. Custom Productivity Tools & Utilities:

- **The Dream:** Creating small, personalized tools perfectly tailored to your specific workflow or needs, things you can't quite find in off-the-shelf software.
- **Vibe Coding Power:** This is a fantastic area for Vibe Coding, leveraging its ability to create functionality based on your descriptions:
    - o **Trackers:** Build simple trackers for habits, moods (like our Chapter 5 example), expenses, workouts, project time, etc. Prompt for input fields, saving mechanisms (like Local Storage), and ways to display the tracked data (lists, simple charts – you can ask the AI to help generate basic charts using JavaScript libraries).
    - o **Calculators:** Need a specific calculation for your work or hobby? A niche financial calculator, a material estimator for crafting, a recipe scaler? Describe the inputs, the formula, and the desired output format to the AI.

- o **Simple Databases/Organizers:** Create tools to collect and organize information – a personal CRM for freelance clients, a database of research notes, a collection of favorite online articles with tags, the movie watchlist from Chapter 5. Prompt for forms to add data, ways to display it (lists, tables), and maybe simple search or filter functionality.
- o **Generators:** Build simple generators – a random writing prompt generator, a workout routine randomizer, a tool to generate color palettes based on certain rules.
- **Example Vibe Coding Scenario:** A freelancer could prompt: "Create a simple 'Project Time Tracker' web app. I need an input field for 'Task Name', a 'Start Timer' button, a 'Stop Timer' button, and an area to display a list of tasks with the time spent on each. When I click Start, it should record the start time. When I click Stop, it should calculate the duration and add the task name and duration to the list below. Use Local Storage to save the list."

5. Basic Games & Interactive Experiences:

- **The Dream:** Bringing a simple game idea to life, creating a fun quiz for your audience, or building a small interactive simulation.
- **Vibe Coding Power:** While complex, graphically intensive games are likely beyond the scope of pure Vibe Coding for beginners, simpler concepts are often achievable:
  - o **Text Adventures:** Use prompts to define rooms, descriptions, choices, and outcomes. The AI can generate the JavaScript logic to manage the game state and display text based on user input.
  - o **Quizzes:** Prompt the AI to create a multiple-choice or true/false quiz structure. Describe how questions and answers should be stored, how scoring should work, and how results should be displayed.
  - o **"Guess the Number" / Simple Logic Games:** Describe the rules of the game, and the AI can generate the logic for generating random numbers, comparing user guesses, providing feedback ("higher," "lower"), and tracking attempts.
  - o **Very Simple Visual Games (with caution):** For something like "Catch the Falling Object," you could *try* prompting for the basic HTML/CSS/JavaScript setup (e.g., using simple shapes, basic movement, click detection), but visual game development often involves complexities (like smooth animation, collision detection) where AI might struggle or produce inefficient code. Start extremely simple here.
- **Example Vibe Coding Scenario:** Someone wanting to create a history quiz could prompt: "Create a simple multiple-choice quiz web page about World War II. Use JavaScript. Store 5 questions and their

possible answers (A, B, C, D) and the correct answer within the script for now. Display one question at a time. When the user selects an answer and clicks 'Next', tell them if they were right or wrong, then show the next question. At the end, display their final score."

6. Automating Simple Personal Tasks:

- **The Dream:** Saving time and effort by automating repetitive digital tasks you perform regularly.
- **Vibe Coding Power:** Depending on the AI tool and platform (some are better suited for generating scripts in languages like Python), you might be able to automate simple tasks:
  - **File Renaming:** "Write a Python script that goes through all the files in a specific folder and renames any file ending in '.jpeg' to end in '.jpg' instead."
  - **Simple Text Processing:** "Write a JavaScript function that takes a paragraph of text and counts how many times the word 'vibe' appears."
  - **Basic Web Scraping (Use Ethically!):** "Write a Python script using the 'requests' and 'BeautifulSoup' libraries to fetch the headlines from the homepage of '[Specific News Website]' and print them to the console." (Note: Web scraping requires care regarding website terms of service and robots.txt files).
  - **Generating Boilerplate:** "Generate the basic HTML structure for a standard webpage, including the doctype, head section with a title, and an empty body tag."
- **Example Vibe Coding Scenario:** Someone needing to clean up photo filenames could prompt (perhaps using an AI integrated with a Python environment): "Write a Python script. It should ask the user for a folder path. Then, it should look at all files in that folder. If a filename contains spaces, it should replace the spaces with underscores ('_')."

This list is not exhaustive, but it illustrates the breadth of possibilities within the Vibe Coding sweet spot. The common thread is leveraging AI to handle the generation of relatively standard code structures and logic based on clear descriptions, enabling creators to build functional and personalized digital tools and experiences much more easily than before.

What Makes a Project "Vibe-Friendly"? Key Factors

Looking at these examples, we can distill the characteristics that often make a project a good fit for Vibe Coding, especially for non-technical creators:

1. **Clear Goal & Vision:** You need to know *what* you want to build, at least at a high level. The AI can't invent your core idea for you. Having a clear purpose helps you write focused prompts and evaluate

the results effectively. If your goal is fuzzy ("I want something cool for music lovers"), it's hard to direct the AI. If it's clear ("I want a tool to list upcoming concerts for specific bands saved by the user"), you have a target.

2. **Manageable Scope (Start Small!):** Trying to build a massive, feature-rich application in one go is a recipe for frustration with any development method, and especially with Vibe Coding. Start with a **Minimum Viable Product (MVP)** – the absolute simplest version of your idea that still delivers core value. For the movie watchlist, the MVP was just adding and viewing titles. Marking as watched and persistence came later. Get the core working first, then iterate and add features one by one. This keeps the process manageable and provides motivating early wins.

3. **Reliance on Standard Features:** Vibe Coding AI excels when leveraging the vast amount of existing code it was trained on. This means projects built primarily from common web elements (text, images, buttons, forms, lists), standard interactions (clicking buttons, submitting forms, displaying data), and relatively straightforward logic (calculations, saving/loading simple data, basic game rules) are often the most successful. The AI has seen countless examples of these and can generate reliable code for them.

If your project idea aligns well with these factors – a clear goal, a scope you can tackle incrementally starting with an MVP, and functionality built mostly from standard patterns – then it's likely a fantastic candidate for Vibe Coding.

Navigating the Boundaries: Understanding Vibe Coding's Limitations

Now, let's talk about the other side of the coin. While Vibe Coding is incredibly empowering, it's not a magic wand capable of effortlessly building *anything* you can imagine, especially not complex, mission-critical software. Understanding its current limitations is crucial for avoiding frustration and using the tool appropriately. Framing these limitations constructively helps us see Vibe Coding not as flawed, but as a specific tool with an optimal range of use – like using a paintbrush for painting, not for hammering nails.

Here are key areas where pure Vibe Coding (relying heavily on AI generation without deep technical understanding or review) can be challenging or risky:

1. Extreme Complexity & Interconnectedness:

- **What it means:** Applications with a vast number of features that interact in intricate ways, involve complex algorithms, manage large and relational datasets, or require real-time synchronization between many users (like a complex multiplayer game or a large-scale enterprise system).

- **Why it's tricky:**
  - **AI Context Limits:** AI models have limits on how much information they can process at once. Managing the intricate dependencies across dozens or hundreds of files and features in a large project can exceed these limits, leading to inconsistent or incorrect code.
  - **Subtle Bugs:** In complex systems, bugs can arise from unexpected interactions between different parts. An AI might generate code for each part that looks correct in isolation, but fails when integrated. Diagnosing these subtle, system-level bugs often requires deep technical understanding that goes beyond describing symptoms.
  - **Architectural Design:** Building complex systems requires careful architectural planning – deciding how different parts should be structured and communicate. While AI can *suggest* architectures, making sound, scalable architectural decisions for large applications still largely relies on human expertise and experience.
- **Analogy:** Vibe Coding might be great for building a functional go-kart quickly by describing the parts. Building a Formula 1 racing car, with its incredibly complex, interconnected systems optimized for extreme performance, requires a different level of deep engineering knowledge and control.
- **Takeaway:** For highly complex applications, Vibe Coding might be useful for prototyping specific features or generating boilerplate, but relying on it solely for the entire development process is likely impractical and risky.

2. High Security Requirements:

- **What it means:** Applications that handle sensitive user data (like login credentials, passwords, financial information, personal health records) or perform critical transactions (like payment processing).
- **Why it's tricky and HIGHLY RISKY:**
  - **Security is Hard:** Building secure software is notoriously difficult, even for experienced human developers. It requires deep knowledge of common vulnerabilities (like cross-site scripting, SQL injection, insecure data storage), best practices, and constant vigilance.
  - **AI is Not a Security Expert:** AI models are trained on vast amounts of code, including potentially insecure code found online. They don't inherently possess a deep understanding of security principles and might generate code with subtle vulnerabilities that a non-expert would never spot.
  - **Consequences are Severe:** A security breach in an application handling sensitive data can have devastating

consequences for users and the creator (legal liability, loss of trust).

- **Analogy:** You wouldn't ask a talented apprentice sculptor, however fast, to design the vault for a national bank. Security requires specialized expertise and rigorous testing beyond just making something *look* like a vault.
- **Takeaway: Do NOT rely solely on Vibe Coding to build systems that handle sensitive data or financial transactions from scratch.** This is non-negotiable. Instead, leverage secure, established third-party services for things like authentication (e.g., using "Sign in with Google" or dedicated services like Auth0), payment processing (Stripe, PayPal), and storing sensitive data. Vibe Coding can help you *integrate* these secure services into your application, but don't try to build the core security yourself this way.

3. High Reliability & Performance Needs:

- **What it means:** Applications where failure or poor performance is unacceptable or has significant consequences. Think medical monitoring software, air traffic control systems (extreme examples), or even just applications that need to handle thousands of simultaneous users without slowing down.
- **Why it's tricky:**
  - **Robustness Requires Rigor:** Building highly reliable software involves meticulous error handling, extensive testing (including edge cases and stress testing), and often performance optimization – practices that require deep understanding and control over the code.
  - **AI Code Can Be Inefficient:** AI might generate code that works functionally but is inefficient ("slow") or doesn't scale well under heavy load. Identifying and fixing performance bottlenecks often requires profiling tools and code optimization skills.
  - **Lack of Deep Understanding:** If you, the creator, don't fully understand the code generated by the AI, it's extremely difficult to guarantee its reliability under all conditions or to optimize its performance effectively.
- **Analogy:** You could vibe code a fun remote-controlled toy car. You wouldn't vibe code the control system for a self-driving car where reliability is a matter of life and death.
- **Takeaway:** For applications where extreme reliability or high performance under load is critical, Vibe Coding alone is insufficient. It might help prototype, but the final product will require rigorous engineering, testing, and optimization, likely involving traditional development practices.

4. Highly Novel or Innovative Features:

- **What it means:** You're trying to build something truly unique, with interactions, algorithms, or features that have few existing precedents for the AI to learn from.
- **Why it's tricky:**
  - **AI Learns from Data:** LLMs primarily learn by identifying patterns in the vast amounts of existing code and text they were trained on. If your idea is radically different from anything it has seen before, it may struggle to generate relevant or effective code. It's better at recombining and adapting existing patterns than inventing entirely new ones from scratch.
  - **Ambiguity of Novelty:** Describing a truly novel concept in a way the AI can understand and translate into code can be extremely difficult.
- **Analogy:** An AI trained on millions of photos of cats and dogs can easily generate a new picture of a cat or a dog. Asking it to generate a picture of an animal that has never existed and follows entirely new biological rules would be much harder.
- **Takeaway:** Vibe Coding is fantastic for building applications based on established patterns (even complex combinations of them) quickly and accessibly. For truly groundbreaking, never-before-seen functionality, it might be less effective. Human ingenuity and potentially traditional coding are often needed to blaze entirely new trails, though AI might still assist in implementing parts of the novel idea once it's better defined.

5. Long-Term Maintainability & Collaboration:

- **What it means:** Thinking about how the application will be updated, fixed, or expanded over months or years, or how easily other people could understand and contribute to it.
- **Why it's tricky:**
  - **The "Black Box" Problem:** If you rely heavily on vibe coding and never delve into understanding the generated code, your application can become a "black box." When a bug appears six months later, or you want to add a complex new feature, debugging or modifying that code base can be incredibly difficult if you don't know how it works internally.
  - **Collaboration Challenges:** Handing off a vibe-coded project to another developer (even another vibe coder) can be hard if the underlying structure and logic aren't well-understood or documented. The original creator's "vibe" and iterative prompting history might be lost.
- **Takeaway:** For projects intended to have a long lifespan or involve multiple collaborators, consider the maintainability implications.

Responsible vibe coding might involve gradually learning more about the generated code, encouraging the AI to add comments, or eventually bringing in technical expertise for review or refactoring if the project grows significantly. For purely personal, short-term tools, this is less of a concern.

Understanding these boundaries isn't meant to discourage you. On the contrary, it's meant to help you succeed by choosing projects where Vibe Coding can truly shine.

Conclusion: Choosing Your Adventure Wisely

Vibe Coding opens up a universe of creative possibilities. You *can* build that portfolio website, that landing page, that custom habit tracker, that simple game, or that handy personal utility – often faster and more easily than ever before. The sweet spot lies in projects with clear goals, manageable scopes (start small!), and reliance on the kinds of standard features and interactions that AI excels at generating.

At the same time, it's crucial to be a mindful creator. Recognize that for applications demanding high complexity, stringent security, guaranteed reliability, or truly groundbreaking innovation, Vibe Coding is likely only one part of the solution, perhaps best used for prototyping or generating initial structures, rather than the sole method for building the entire finished product. And always consider the security implications – never try to vibe code sensitive systems like payment processing from scratch.

Think of Vibe Coding as an incredibly versatile and powerful new tool in your creative toolkit. Like any tool, it has jobs it's perfectly suited for and jobs where a different tool (like traditional coding, no-code platforms, or secure third-party services) might be more appropriate.

Our journey through Vibe Coding is about empowerment. Part of that empowerment comes from understanding not just the potential, but also the responsible application of these amazing new capabilities. Choose your first projects wisely. Start with something in the sweet spot. Build your confidence, practice your prompting skills, and experience the thrill of bringing your ideas to life. As you grow more comfortable, you can gradually tackle more ambitious projects, always keeping the capabilities and limitations of your AI co-creator in mind.

Now that you know what you *can* build and how to approach it, there's one more crucial piece: how to do it *responsibly*. Let's talk about safety, testing, and mindful creation in the next chapter.

A.K.Nayak

CHAPTER 8: STAYING SAFE AND SMART: RESPONSIBLE VIBING

This Chapter Covers

Focus: Using Vibe Coding safely/smartly by understanding risks & adopting good habits.

Potential Risks:
- **Hidden Bugs:** Code fails on edge cases.
- **Security Issues:** Vulnerabilities, **critical risk** for sensitive data.
- **Maintenance Difficulty:** Code becomes hard-to-understand "black box".

Responsible Vibing Habits:
1. **Test Thoroughly & Often:** Crucial for quality; include edge cases.
2. **Start Small & Simple:** Build incrementally (MVP first).
3. **Handle Sensitive Data Securely: Use 3rd-party services** for logins/payments; **never** build from scratch.
4. **Save Work Often:** Use backups/versioning.
5. **Consider AI 'Second Opinion':** Ask another AI to review code.
6. **Don't Trust Blindly:** Use critical thinking & test results.

Goal: Empower safe, effective creation through awareness & good practices.

> *"With great power comes great responsibility."*
>
> **— Uncle Ben**

By now, you've hopefully felt the surge of excitement that comes with Vibe Coding. You've seen how conversation and intuition, guided by powerful AI tools, can transform your ideas into working applications. You've walked through the process, learned how to communicate your vision through prompts, and explored the kinds of cool projects you can build. It truly feels like a new era of digital creation is dawning, one where your ideas are the main currency.

This newfound power is exhilarating. But like any powerful tool – whether it's a car, a kitchen knife, or even the internet itself – using it effectively and safely involves understanding how it works, being aware of potential risks, and adopting some sensible practices. This isn't about dampening your enthusiasm; it's about channeling it productively and ensuring your creative journey is smooth, sustainable, and free from unnecessary bumps or hazards.

Think of it like learning to drive. The first thrill is making the car move, turning the wheel, feeling the speed. But true confidence and enjoyment come when you also understand the rules of the road, how to check your mirrors, when to brake safely, and how to handle unexpected situations. This chapter is about learning the "rules of the road" for Vibe Coding.

We need to be honest: AI, while incredible, is not perfect. The code generated by your AI co-creator won't always be flawless. Sometimes it might misunderstand you, sometimes it might take shortcuts you didn't intend, and sometimes it might just make mistakes, drawing on the vast but imperfect sea of information it was trained on. Relying on code you didn't write and might not fully understand introduces unique challenges.

But don't let that scare you! By understanding these potential issues upfront and adopting a few straightforward, practical habits – what we'll call **Responsible Vibing** – you can navigate these challenges confidently. This chapter is dedicated to empowering you with that awareness and those habits. It's about ensuring your Vibe Coding experience is not just exciting, but also safe, smart, and ultimately more successful.

Understanding the Potential Road Bumps: Common Risks in Vibe Coding

Before we dive into the good habits, let's clearly understand the main types of issues you might encounter when relying heavily on AI-generated code, especially without a deep technical background. Awareness is the first step towards mitigation.

1. Hidden Bugs: The Gremlins in the Machine

- **What it means:** This is perhaps the most common issue. The AI generates code, you test the main functionality, and it seems to work perfectly! You celebrate, maybe even start using your new app. But later, under slightly different circumstances, something goes wrong. Maybe the app crashes when you enter text with a specific symbol (like an apostrophe, as in our Chapter 5 example). Maybe a calculation is wrong, but only for certain numbers. Maybe a feature works fine for the first few times but then stops working correctly. These are hidden bugs – problems lurking beneath the surface that didn't show up in your initial tests.
- **Why it happens:** AI models learn patterns from millions of code examples, but they don't truly *understand* the underlying logic or the infinite ways users might interact with software. They might generate code that covers the most common cases but fails on edge cases (unusual inputs or situations). They might combine code snippets in ways that create subtle conflicts. Sometimes, the code they learned from was itself buggy.

- **Analogy:** Imagine an AI chef giving you a recipe. It works perfectly 9 times out of 10. But the AI forgot to mention that if you use a specific brand of flour (an edge case), the cake won't rise properly. The core recipe seems fine, but a hidden flaw exists under specific conditions.
- **The Risk:** Hidden bugs can range from minor annoyances to major problems that make your app unusable or produce incorrect results, undermining its value and potentially frustrating users (even if the only user is you).

2. Security Issues: Leaving the Digital Door Unlocked

- **What it means:** This is a more serious category of risk, particularly if your application handles any kind of information entered by users or fetched from elsewhere. Security issues are vulnerabilities that could allow unauthorized individuals to access data, misuse your application, inject malicious code, or cause other harm.
- **Why it happens:** Building secure software is a specialized skill. AI models, trained on publicly available code (which includes plenty of insecure examples), are generally **not** security experts. They might generate code that:
  - Doesn't properly validate user input (allowing malicious scripts to be entered).
  - Stores information insecurely (e.g., putting sensitive data in easily accessible places like Local Storage without protection).
  - Connects to other services without proper safeguards.
  - Includes outdated components with known vulnerabilities.
- **Analogy:** Imagine asking an AI to design a door for your house based on pictures of thousands of doors. It might design a beautiful door that looks sturdy, but it might forget to include a lock, or it might use a type of lock known to be easily picked, simply because it saw many examples like that. It focused on the appearance and basic function (opening/closing) but missed the critical security aspect.
- **The Risk:** Security vulnerabilities can be exploited to steal data, deface websites, spread malware, or spam users. Even for simple personal tools, poor security (like storing personal notes insecurely) can lead to privacy breaches. **For any application handling logins, payments, or sensitive personal data, the security risks of using unvetted, AI-generated code are extremely high.**

3. Maintenance Difficulty: The Mysterious Black Box

- **What it means:** You've successfully vibe coded an application. It works! But six months later, a bug appears, or you want to add a significant new feature. You open up the project (or look at the code files), and... you have very little idea how it actually works internally. The AI generated it through conversation, but the underlying logic and structure might be complex or non-intuitive. It's become a "black box" – you know what goes in and what comes out, but the inner workings are a mystery.

- **Why it happens:** This is inherent in the Vibe Coding process if you rely solely on prompting and testing without making an effort to understand the generated code. The AI prioritizes fulfilling your prompt, not necessarily creating the cleanest, most understandable, or most maintainable code structure (though you can prompt for clarity!). The conversational history might be lost, leaving only the final code.
- **Analogy:** Imagine someone gifts you a complex, custom-built machine that performs a useful task. It works great initially. But when it breaks down, you have no blueprints, no manual, and the original builder is gone. Trying to fix it by randomly poking at wires is incredibly difficult and likely to make things worse.
- **The Risk:** Code that isn't understood is extremely hard to debug effectively when problems arise later. Adding new features can become a nightmare, as you might inadvertently break existing functionality without realizing it. Collaborating with others, or handing the project off, becomes very challenging. This "technical debt" can eventually make the application impossible to maintain or evolve.

Acknowledging these risks isn't about giving up on Vibe Coding. Far from it! It's about recognizing where we need to be careful and proactive. Forewarned is forearmed. Now, let's focus on the practical habits – the "Responsible Vibing" techniques – that help mitigate these risks and make your creative process safer and more robust.

Responsible Vibing Tip 1: Test, Test, Test (Become a Master Tester)

If there's one golden rule in Vibe Coding, this is it. Since you might not understand every line of code the AI writes, rigorous testing becomes your primary method for ensuring quality, catching bugs (even hidden ones), and verifying that the application actually does what you intend. Don't think of testing as a chore; think of it as a core part of the creative process – it's how you confirm your vision is being realized correctly.

We're not talking about complex, automated software testing frameworks here (unless you want to learn!). We're focusing on **Functional Testing** from a user's perspective: Does the app *do* what it's supposed to do, correctly and reliably, under various conditions?

- **Adopt a Tester's Mindset:** Don't just test the "happy path" (the normal, expected way someone would use the app). Actively try to explore edge cases and even gently try to "break" things. What happens if...?

- **Test After Every Significant Change:** Got the AI to add a new feature or fix a bug? **Test it immediately.** Don't batch up multiple changes before testing. This makes it much easier to pinpoint the source if something goes wrong. Did the "Remove" button feature break the "Mark as Watched" feature? You'll know right away if you test after adding "Remove".
- **Be Systematic (Use a Mental Checklist):**
  - **Test Inputs:**
    - *Normal Values:* Enter typical data (e.g., movie titles, numbers in a calculator).
    - *Empty Values:* What happens if you leave a required field blank and click submit? Does it handle it gracefully (e.g., show a message) or crash?
    - *Boundary Values:* If dealing with numbers, try zero, negative numbers, very large numbers.
    - *Different Data Types:* If expecting a number, what if you type text?
    - *Special Characters:* Try inputs with apostrophes, quotes, symbols (&, $, <, >). Does it handle them correctly or cause display issues or errors? (Remember the apostrophe bug example).
    - *Long Inputs:* What if you type a very long movie title or note? Does it display correctly or break the layout?
  - **Test Core Logic:**
    - *Calculations:* Double-check any math the app does with a separate calculator. Try multiple different inputs.
    - *Saving/Loading:* Does data persist correctly after refreshing or closing/reopening (if using Local Storage or similar)? Add data, change data, delete data, then refresh and verify.
    - *State Changes:* Does marking an item as "watched" actually stick? Does toggling work if you implemented it? Does completing a task update a progress bar correctly?
  - **Test User Flows:**
    - Go through the entire sequence of actions a user would take. Can you successfully add a movie, mark it watched, and then remove it? Can you complete the quiz from start to finish?
    - Try navigating between different sections or pages (if applicable). Do links work? Does the state remain consistent?
  - **Test Interactions:**

- *Button Clicks:* Click buttons multiple times quickly. Does it cause problems (like adding duplicate items)?
- *Combinations:* Try using features in different orders. Does marking as watched before saving cause issues?
- **Document Bugs (Simply):** If you find a bug, make a quick note of *exactly* what you did and *exactly* what happened. This will be crucial for writing a clear error description prompt for the AI (Tip #6).

Analogy: Think of testing like proofreading an important document multiple times. The first read catches obvious typos. The second read checks grammar. The third read checks for logical flow and clarity. Thorough testing of your vibe-coded app requires looking at it from different angles to catch various kinds of potential issues.

Testing is your quality control. It's your way of verifying the work of your AI apprentice. Don't skimp on it! Diligent testing after each step is the single best way to catch bugs early and build confidence in your creation.

Responsible Vibing Tip 2: Start Small & Simple (Build Incrementally)

We touched on this when discussing project scope, but it's also a fundamental safety principle. Trying to vibe code a huge, complex application right out of the gate is like trying to learn skiing by starting on a black diamond slope – you're likely to fall, get frustrated, and potentially give up.

- **Why Start Small is Safer:**
    - **Fewer Moving Parts:** Simpler applications have less code and fewer interacting components, meaning fewer places for hidden bugs or security issues to lurk.
    - **Easier to Test:** Thoroughly testing a small application with limited features is much more feasible than trying to test a sprawling one.
    - **Easier to Understand (Relatively):** Even if you don't read the code, grasping the overall flow and logic of a simple app is easier, making troubleshooting less daunting.
    - **Builds Confidence:** Successfully completing a small project provides a huge confidence boost and practical experience with the Vibe Coding process, preparing you for slightly more complex endeavors later.
- **The MVP Mindset:** Embrace the concept of the Minimum Viable Product (MVP). What is the absolute simplest version of your idea that delivers core value? Build *that* first. Get it working reliably. Test it thoroughly. *Then*, incrementally add the next most important feature, testing again after each addition.
- **Analogy:** Learn to cook by mastering scrambled eggs before attempting a complex Beef Wellington. Learn to swim in the shallow

end before venturing into deep water. Build your Vibe Coding skills and confidence on smaller, manageable projects first.

Resist the urge to prompt the AI with a massive list of features for Version 1. Start with the core, get it right, test it well, and then build outwards. This incremental approach is not only more manageable but also inherently safer.

Responsible Vibing Tip 3: Be Extremely Careful with Sensitive Data (Know the Danger Zone)

This point cannot be stressed enough, especially for non-technical creators. Handling sensitive data improperly is one of the biggest risks associated with building software, regardless of how it's built.

- **What is Sensitive Data?** Anything that could cause harm or embarrassment if exposed. This includes, but is not limited to:
    - User passwords
    - Credit card numbers, bank account details
    - Private health information
    - Social Security numbers or other government IDs
    - Private messages or journals
    - Any personally identifiable information (PII) that isn't explicitly public (e.g., home addresses, phone numbers, potentially even email addresses if stored insecurely alongside other data).
- **The Golden Rule: Do NOT attempt to build systems that directly handle, store, or process highly sensitive data like passwords or payment information using Vibe Coding alone, without expert security review.** The risk of the AI generating insecure code is simply too high, and the consequences of a breach are too severe.
- **Safer Alternatives (Your Go-To Solutions):**
    - **For Logins/Authentication:** NEVER store passwords yourself. Use established, secure third-party authentication providers. Examples:
        - **Social Logins:** "Sign in with Google," "Sign in with Apple," etc. These are secure and convenient for users. You can prompt your AI: "Help me integrate the 'Sign in with Google' button using their official JavaScript library."
        - **Dedicated Services:** Platforms like Auth0, Firebase Authentication, Supabase Auth specialize in providing secure user login and management. Prompt the AI: "Show me how to add user signup and login using Firebase Authentication to my web app."
    - **For Payments:** NEVER handle credit card numbers directly. Use reputable payment processors. Examples:

- **Payment Links/Buttons:** Stripe Checkout, PayPal Buttons, Gumroad provide secure, hosted pages or simple buttons to handle payments. Prompt the AI: "Help me add a Stripe Checkout button to my product page. Here is the button code snippet provided by Stripe..."
  - **For Storing Other Potentially Sensitive Data:** If your app needs to store user data beyond simple preferences (which might be okay in Local Storage for *personal*, non-shared tools), consider using secure backend database services that offer proper security rules and access controls (like Google's Firebase Firestore or Supabase's database). Prompt the AI for help *integrating* with the official libraries (APIs) for these services, rather than trying to build your own database logic.
- **Local Storage Caveat:** While we used Local Storage in the movie watchlist for persistence, understand its limitations. Data in Local Storage is stored directly in the user's browser, is not encrypted by default, and can potentially be accessed by other scripts running on the same domain (though modern browsers have safeguards). It's generally okay for non-sensitive data in personal tools (like a movie list, theme preference, simple game score) but **not suitable** for passwords, private notes, or anything truly confidential, especially if the app might be shared or used by others. When in doubt, err on the side of caution.

Protecting user data is paramount. Always prioritize using secure, established third-party services for handling anything sensitive. Use Vibe Coding to build your unique features and integrate these services, not to reinvent insecure wheels.

Responsible Vibing Tip 4: Save Your Work Often (Create Safety Nets)

Imagine spending hours perfecting your project through prompts, only for your browser to crash or the AI platform to have a temporary glitch, losing all your progress. Or imagine the AI generates code that completely breaks your application, and you wish you could go back to the version that worked just five minutes ago. Saving frequently creates essential safety nets.

- **Why Save Often?**
  - **Protects Against Loss:** Hardware failures, software crashes, internet issues, accidental deletions – saving protects your work.
  - **Enables Rollback:** If a new feature or AI-suggested change introduces major problems, having a recent saved version allows you to easily revert back to a known working state without starting over.

- o **Supports Experimentation:** Knowing you can easily go back to a stable version encourages experimentation. You can try prompting for a risky feature, knowing you can undo it if it doesn't work out.
- **Simple Versioning Strategies (No Complex Tools Needed Initially):**
    - o **Manual "Save As":** The simplest method. Periodically (e.g., after getting a significant feature working), save a complete copy of your project folder or files. Name the copies clearly with dates or version numbers: MovieWatchlist_v1_BasicAdd, MovieWatchlist_v2_MarkAsWatched, MovieWatchlist_v3_PersistenceFix, MovieWatchlist_2025-04-17. This is easy to do but can become cluttered over time.
    - o **Platform Features:** Check if the platform you're using (like Replit) has built-in version history or a "fork" feature. Replit often automatically saves snapshots of your code history, allowing you to browse and restore previous versions – explore these features! Forking creates a completely separate copy of your project, which is great for trying major changes without affecting the original.
    - o **Cloud Storage Sync:** Using services like Dropbox, Google Drive, or OneDrive to store your project files can provide automatic backups and sometimes basic version history.
    - o **Git (The Professional Standard - Optional Later Step):** For larger projects or collaboration, learning a version control system like Git (often used with GitHub or GitLab) is invaluable. It allows detailed tracking of changes, branching (working on features independently), merging, and easy rollbacks. While Git has a learning curve, it's the industry standard for a reason. You don't need it to start Vibe Coding, but be aware of it as a powerful option if your projects grow more serious.
- **Analogy:** Think of it like hitting "Save" frequently while writing a document, or keeping backup copies of important photos on a separate drive. It's a simple habit that can prevent major headaches.

Get into the habit of saving stable checkpoints of your work. Before prompting for a major new feature or fix, consider saving a copy or ensuring your platform has saved a recent version. Your future self will thank you!

Responsible Vibing Tip 5: Consider a 'Second Opinion' (AI Peer Review)

Your primary AI assistant is working hard, generating code based on your prompts. But is the code any good? Is it efficient? Does it have potential issues you haven't spotted through testing? One interesting technique emerging in the Vibe Coding space is to get a "second opinion" from *another* AI tool.

- **How it Works:** You take a snippet of code (or even a whole file) generated by your primary AI (let's call it AI-1) and paste it into the chat window of a different AI model (AI-2, maybe from a different company like ChatGPT if you were using Claude, or vice-versa). Then you ask AI-2 to review it.
- **Example Prompts for a Second Opinion:**
  - "Can you review this JavaScript code generated by another AI? Please look for any potential bugs, inefficiencies, or security concerns a beginner might miss."
  - "Does this HTML structure follow good accessibility practices (like using proper tags, alt text for images, etc.)?"
  - "This function calculates the average of a list of numbers. Is there a simpler or more standard way to write this in Python?"
  - "I asked an AI to add error handling to this form submission code. Does this look like a reasonable approach?"
- **Benefits:**
  - **Catching Obvious Errors:** A second AI might spot mistakes or bad practices that the first AI missed.
  - **Different Perspectives:** Different AI models might have different strengths or training data, potentially offering alternative, sometimes better, ways of doing things.
  - **Learning Opportunity:** Reading the second AI's critique or suggestions can be another way to learn about code quality and best practices.
- **Caveats:**
  - **Not Foolproof:** The second AI is also not perfect and might miss issues or even introduce new ones with its suggestions.
  - **Conflicting Advice:** You might get conflicting opinions or stylistic suggestions from different AIs. You'll still need to use your judgment (and testing!) to decide which advice to follow.
- **Analogy:** It's like asking a colleague to quickly proofread an email before you send it, or getting a second opinion from another doctor before a major procedure. It's an extra check that might catch something important.

Using a second AI for review isn't a replacement for thorough testing, but it can be a helpful supplementary step, especially if you're feeling unsure about a particular piece of generated code.

Responsible Vibing Tip 6: Don't Trust Blindly (Engage Your Critical Thinking)

This final principle underpins all the others. Perhaps the biggest mental shift required for responsible Vibe Coding is moving from passively accepting the

AI's output to actively, critically engaging with it. The AI is an incredibly powerful tool, but it is still just a tool. **You are the creator, the director, the one ultimately responsible for the final product.**

- **Question the Output:** Don't assume the AI's first answer is always the best or only answer.
    - *Ask yourself:* Does this generated code *actually* solve the problem I described? Does the explanation make sense? Does the suggested approach feel right for my project's goals and vibe?
- **Look for "AI Hallucinations":** Be aware that LLMs can sometimes "hallucinate" – confidently state incorrect information or generate code that refers to non-existent functions or libraries. If something sounds too good to be true or seems overly complex/strange, be skeptical. Verify through testing or ask clarifying questions.
- **Use Your Common Sense:** If the AI generates text content for your app, read it critically. Does it sound natural? Is it grammatically correct? Does it fit the tone you want? The AI is good, but your human judgment is still needed.
- **Trust Your Domain Expertise:** If you're building a tool related to your field (baking, art, finance, education), and the AI suggests logic or content that contradicts your expert knowledge, trust your expertise! The AI might not understand the nuances of your specific domain. Push back, correct it, or refine the prompt based on what you know to be true.
- **Testing as the Ultimate Truth Serum:** When in doubt, test! Testing the actual behavior of the application is the best way to cut through potential AI errors or misunderstandings and see what's really going on.

Analogy: Think of using GPS navigation. It's an amazing tool, but you don't follow it blindly off a cliff or down a clearly closed road. You keep your eyes on the actual road, use your common sense, question directions that seem wrong, and remain aware of your surroundings. Treat your AI co-creator the same way – leverage its guidance, but keep your critical thinking engaged.

Blind trust is risky. Healthy skepticism, combined with thorough testing and common sense, is the path to using these tools effectively and safely.

Conclusion: Empowerment Through Awareness

Vibe Coding offers a thrilling path to creation, breaking down long-standing technical barriers. But like any journey into new territory, it's wise to travel with awareness and good preparation. Understanding the potential risks – hidden bugs, security vulnerabilities, and maintenance challenges – isn't meant to deter you, but to equip you.

By embracing the practices of Responsible Vibing:

- **Testing diligently** after every step,
- **Starting with simple, manageable projects**,
- **Handling sensitive data with extreme caution** (using third-party services),
- **Saving your work frequently**,
- **Considering AI "second opinions"** when needed, and crucially,
- **Maintaining your critical thinking** and not trusting blindly,

...you transform Vibe Coding from a potentially risky experiment into a sustainable, empowering, and incredibly rewarding creative process. These habits aren't restrictive; they are liberating. They give you the confidence to explore, experiment, and build, knowing you have strategies to navigate the challenges along the way.

You have the vision, you have the tools, and now you have the awareness to use them smartly and safely. The digital canvas awaits your unique touch. Go forth and vibe responsibly!

CHAPTER 9: THE FUTURE IS VIBEY: WHAT'S NEXT?

This Chapter Covers

Focus: Future evolution of Vibe Coding and its impact.
Future Trends:
1. **Smarter AI:** Better understanding, code quality, debugging; multi-modal input (voice/sketch).
2. **Natural Interaction:** Voice interfaces, multi-modal prompts, increased accessibility.
3. **Democratization:** More creators, hyper-personalization, niche innovation.

Evolving Creator Skills: Emphasis shifts to Vision, Communication (Prompting), Creativity, Critical Evaluation/Testing, Ethics; less on manual coding.
Outlook: Digital creation becomes more accessible; success relies on vision, communication & critical thinking. Encourages participation.

> *"The empires of the future are the empires of the mind."*
>
> *- Winston Churchill*

We've journeyed together through the landscape of Vibe Coding as it exists today. We've demystified the concept, met the AI tools acting as our co-creators, walked through the practical steps of building an application via conversation, learned the art of crafting effective prompts, explored the kinds of projects that fit well within this paradigm, and discussed how to approach it all responsibly. You now possess the foundational understanding and, hopefully, the growing confidence to start turning your own unique ideas into digital reality.

But the story of Vibe Coding is far from over. In fact, we are standing at the very beginning of a potentially transformative shift in how humans create with technology. The AI tools we use today, as impressive as they are, are merely the early prototypes of what's likely to come. The pace of advancement in Artificial Intelligence is breathtaking, and its impact on creative fields, including software development, is only just starting to unfold.

So, what does the future hold? What might Vibe Coding look like in five years? Ten years? What new possibilities will open up for creators like you? While predicting the future is always speculative, we can look at the current trends and extrapolate, painting an inspiring picture of where this journey might lead. This chapter is our peek over the horizon, an exploration of the exciting potential that lies ahead, and a reflection on how your role as a creator might evolve in this increasingly "vibey" future.

Trend 1: Your AI Co-Creator Gets a Major Upgrade (Smarter, More Capable Tools)

The AI assistants we use today are already remarkably capable, but they are constantly learning and improving. The underlying Large Language Models are becoming larger, trained on more diverse data, and equipped with more sophisticated algorithms. This relentless progress points towards a future where our AI co-creators will be significantly smarter, more context-aware, and more helpful.

- **Deeper Understanding:** Future AI might move beyond just understanding the literal meaning of your prompts to grasping the deeper context, nuance, and even unspoken assumptions behind your requests. Imagine an AI that doesn't just follow instructions but anticipates your needs, understands your personal style or brand identity based on previous projects, and asks clarifying questions that demonstrate genuine insight into your goals. It might recognize ambiguity in your prompt and proactively suggest different interpretations or options, rather than just making its best guess.
- **Improved Code Quality & Reliability:** As AI models are trained on better-curated datasets and learn more about software engineering best practices, the quality and reliability of the code they generate are likely to improve. They might become better at avoiding common bugs, writing more efficient code, automatically incorporating basic security measures (though expert oversight for sensitive applications will likely always be necessary), and generating code that is inherently easier to understand and maintain (perhaps by automatically adding clear comments or following consistent structures). This could significantly reduce the burden of testing and debugging, especially for common tasks.
- **Enhanced Debugging & Troubleshooting:** Imagine an AI that doesn't just react to error messages you paste but can actively monitor your application as you test it, pinpointing the likely source of a bug based on observed behavior, and suggesting targeted fixes with clear explanations. It might even be able to automatically propose and test potential solutions for common problems, significantly speeding up the troubleshooting process.
- **More Proactive & Creative Suggestions:** Today's AI mostly reacts to your prompts. Future AI might become more of a proactive

creative partner. It could analyze your project goals and suggest relevant features you hadn't considered, offer different UI design options based on your stated "vibe," point out potential user experience issues, or even generate alternative visual styles for you to choose from. It might move from being just an executor to being a genuine brainstorming partner.

- **Multi-Modal Understanding:** The interaction might move beyond just text. Imagine sketching a rough layout on a tablet and having the AI translate it into HTML and CSS structure. Or describing a user flow verbally and having the AI generate the necessary code and interface elements. AI models are rapidly learning to process and connect information from different modalities (text, images, audio, potentially even video or gestures), opening up more intuitive ways to express your creative intent.

- **Better Handling of Complexity:** While complex systems might remain challenging, future AI could become much better at managing larger projects. They might develop improved "memory" (larger context windows), better capabilities for understanding the relationships between different parts of an application, and tools for visualizing project architecture, making it feasible to vibe code more ambitious projects than is practical today.

Scenario: Vibe Coding in 5 Years (Hypothetical)

Imagine wanting to build that "Personal Movie Watchlist" again, but five years from now:

- *You (speaking to your device):* "Hey AI, let's start a new project. I want a simple web app called 'My Ultimate Film Log' to track movies I want to watch and ones I've seen. The vibe should be minimalist but visually engaging, maybe using movie poster thumbnails. Use my preferred stack: HTML, CSS, modern JavaScript."

- *AI (responding, perhaps visually showing structure):* "Got it. Setting up 'My Ultimate Film Log'. I'll use a clean, card-based layout for the movie list, pulling poster thumbnails automatically when you add a title. Based on your previous projects, I assume you'll want persistence via Local Storage and basic sorting options? And for the 'minimalist but engaging' vibe, I suggest a dark theme with subtle hover effects on the movie cards. How does that sound as a starting point?"

- *You:* "That sounds perfect, especially the dark theme and poster idea! Let's start with just adding titles and displaying the list with posters."

- *AI:* "Okay, generating the initial structure and the JavaScript to fetch poster thumbnails from a public movie database API when a title is added... Done. Here's the preview link. I've also added basic error handling in case a poster isn't found."

Notice the difference? The future AI anticipates needs based on past behavior, proactively suggests design choices aligned with the "vibe," handles external data fetching (like movie posters) more automatically, and even incorporates basic error handling without explicit prompting. The interaction becomes less about detailed instruction and more about high-level direction and confirmation.

Trend 2: Towards Truly Natural Creation (Conversational & Beyond)

As AI gets better at understanding us, the way we interact with it to create will likely become much more natural and intuitive, moving beyond typed commands towards seamless conversation and potentially other modalities.

- **Voice as a Primary Interface:** Many people find speaking more natural and faster than typing. Future Vibe Coding environments might heavily feature voice interaction. Imagine leaning back, describing the feature you want, asking questions, and refining the design through spoken dialogue with your AI assistant. Tools like SuperWhisper, mentioned by Andrej Karpathy, already hint at this direction, allowing voice commands to drive AI coding tools. This could make the process feel even more like collaborating with a human partner.
- **Multi-Modal Prompting:** As mentioned earlier, combining different types of input could become common. You might sketch a UI element on a screen, circle a part of the preview window and say "Change this color to red," or even use hand gestures in a mixed-reality environment to manipulate virtual components while describing the desired logic. The goal is to allow you to express your intent in whatever way feels most natural to you, breaking down the barriers between thought and digital creation.
- **AI as an Ambient Partner:** Instead of explicitly opening a specific tool or chat window, AI assistance might become more integrated into our digital environments. Perhaps an AI passively observes your work (with permission, of course!), anticipates needs, and offers suggestions contextually. It might feel less like using a distinct "tool" and more like having a helpful presence ready to assist when needed.
- **Greater Accessibility:** These shifts towards more natural interaction, particularly voice, hold immense potential for increasing accessibility. People with physical disabilities that make typing difficult, or those with visual impairments, could potentially engage in complex digital creation through voice commands and audio feedback, opening up opportunities previously unavailable.

The ultimate aim is to make the process of translating an idea into a digital reality as frictionless as possible. The "interface" might start to fade into the background, allowing you to focus purely on your creative vision and converse it into existence.

Trend 3: The Explosion of Creators (Democratization Unleashed)

Perhaps the most profound implication of these advancing trends is the continued **democratization of digital creation**. If building software becomes significantly easier, requiring less specialized technical knowledge and relying more on natural language and vision, what happens?

- **Millions of New Creators:** We could see an explosion of people building their own software. Individuals creating hyper-personalized tools perfectly tailored to their unique needs ("software for one"). Hobbyists bringing niche game ideas or community projects to life. Small businesses creating custom internal tools or specialized customer-facing apps without massive development budgets. Domain experts (teachers, scientists, artists, healthcare workers) directly building tools for their fields based on their deep understanding of the real-world problems.
- **Hyper-Personalization:** Forget one-size-fits-all software. Imagine a world where individuals routinely create small apps or scripts to automate parts of their job, manage their personal information exactly how they like, or explore creative ideas digitally, just as easily as they might write a document today. Software becomes less of a monolithic product and more of a personalized, adaptable environment.
- **Niche Innovation:** Large software companies often focus on broad markets. Empowering individuals and small groups allows for the creation of tools and experiences serving highly specific niches or communities that were previously overlooked because the market size didn't justify traditional development costs. Think specialized tools for obscure hobbies, hyper-local community platforms, or aids for specific learning challenges.
- **Innovation from Unexpected Places:** Groundbreaking ideas often come from the intersection of different fields. When domain experts can directly build or prototype their own digital tools without needing to translate their vision through a technical intermediary, the potential for novel solutions based on deep, real-world understanding increases dramatically. A biologist might build a custom data visualization tool; a historian might create an interactive map; a chef might develop a dynamic recipe adaptation app.

This isn't just about making existing software development faster; it's about fundamentally changing *who* can create software and *what* kinds of software get created. It's about unlocking the latent creative potential currently held back by technical barriers.

The Evolving Creator: Your Skills in the Vibey Future

If AI handles more of the actual code writing, does that mean human skills become obsolete? Absolutely not! It means the *emphasis* shifts. The skills required to be an effective creator in an AI-powered future evolve, playing directly to the strengths many non-technical creators already possess.

Here's what likely becomes even *more* valuable:

1. **Vision & Ideation:** The ability to conceive of valuable, useful, or interesting digital ideas remains fundamentally human. What problem needs solving? What experience needs creating? What information needs organizing? AI can help build, but the initial spark, the core concept, comes from you. Knowing your audience, understanding their needs, and having a clear vision for what you want to achieve becomes paramount.

2. **Clear Communication & Prompting:** As we explored in Chapter 6, communicating your intent clearly to the AI is crucial. This skill will only become more important. It involves not just clarity, but also the ability to break down complexity, provide context, describe subjective qualities (the "vibe"), and ask insightful questions. It's about mastering the language of collaboration with AI.

3. **Creativity & Design Thinking:** While AI might generate designs or suggest features, the overarching creative direction, the aesthetic sensibility, the focus on user experience, and the empathy for the end-user remain human domains. You guide the "vibe." You decide what makes an application not just functional, but delightful, intuitive, and engaging. Skills in visual design, user experience (UX) principles, and storytelling become even more relevant.

4. **Critical Evaluation & Testing:** As AI becomes more capable, the temptation to trust it blindly might increase. However, the ability to critically evaluate the AI's output becomes even *more* vital. Does the generated app *actually* meet the user's needs? Is it reliable? Does it function correctly under various conditions? Does it *feel* right? Your judgment, common sense, and diligent testing (as discussed in Chapter 8) are irreplaceable quality control mechanisms. You need to be the discerning Director reviewing the AI's work.

5. **Problem Decomposition:** The skill of taking a large, complex idea and breaking it down into smaller, manageable, logical steps that can be prompted and tested incrementally will remain essential for tackling anything beyond the simplest projects.

6. **Iterative Mindset:** Comfort with experimentation, viewing "failures" as learning opportunities, providing feedback, and gradually refining the creation through multiple cycles remains core to the Vibe Coding process.

7. **Ethical Awareness & Responsibility:** As creation becomes easier, understanding the potential impact of what you build becomes more important. Considering user privacy, accessibility, potential biases in

AI output, and the responsible use of technology are crucial aspects of being a modern creator.

Notice how these skills – vision, communication, creativity, critical thinking, problem-solving, iteration, ethics – are not tied to specific programming languages. They are fundamental creative and strategic competencies. Vibe Coding doesn't eliminate the need for skill; it shifts the focus towards these more inherently human capabilities, allowing you to leverage your strengths in new ways. The "developer" of the future might look less like someone hunched over lines of cryptic code and more like a director, an architect, or a conductor orchestrating AI assistants to realize a creative vision.

A Future Built by You

The trajectory is clear: AI tools for creation will continue to get smarter, interaction will become more natural, and the barriers to building digital tools and experiences will continue to fall. This opens up a future brimming with possibilities, one where digital creation is not the exclusive domain of traditionally trained programmers, but a medium accessible to anyone with an idea and the ability to articulate it.

Imagine the innovation that can be unleashed when a teacher can easily build a custom learning game for their students, when a community organizer can quickly create a platform to coordinate local efforts, when an artist can design an interactive experience to accompany their work, when you can finally build that niche tool you've always wished existed.

This future isn't guaranteed, and it won't be without challenges. We'll need to continue developing best practices for responsible AI use, navigate ethical considerations, and adapt our educational and professional structures. But the potential for empowerment and widespread creativity is undeniable.

This book has aimed to give you the foundational knowledge and confidence to step into this future *today*. The tools may evolve, the interfaces may change, but the core principles of Vibe Coding – articulating vision, communicating clearly, testing rigorously, iterating thoughtfully, and creating responsibly – will remain relevant.

Don't be a passive observer of this technological shift. Be an active participant. Embrace the tools, hone your communication skills, trust your creative instincts, and start building. The future of digital creation is becoming more conversational, more intuitive, more *vibey*. And it's a future that you, with your unique ideas and perspective, have the power to shape.

The next chapter is just a short conclusion, a final word of encouragement as you embark on your own Vibe Coding adventures. The real journey starts now. Go forth and create!

CHAPTER 10: GO CREATE! FINDING YOUR OWN VIBE

This Chapter Covers

- **Core Message:** Vibe Coding empowers non-technical creators.
- **Recap:** Book covered the Vibe Coding journey (concept to responsible use).
- **Essential Balance:** Use Vibe Coding's power responsibly (test, secure data, start simple, think critically).
- **Call to Action: Start experimenting now!** Don't wait for perfection.
- **Getting Started:** Pick a tool, try the sample project (Ch 5), build a very simple personal MVP.
- **Mindset:** Learn by doing; value your ideas.
- **Next Steps:** Choose tool, try sample, brainstorm, prompt, explore communities.

"Do not wait; the time will never be 'just right.' Start where you stand, and work with whatever tools you may have at your command, and better tools will be found as you go along."

- George Herbert

And so, we arrive at the end of our journey together through the exciting world of Vibe Coding – at least, the end of this introductory guide. We started by acknowledging the frustration of having brilliant ideas locked away by technical barriers, and we've explored how a new wave of Artificial Intelligence is dramatically changing the landscape of digital creation.

The core message, the takeaway I hope resonates most strongly, is this: ***Vibe Coding is real, it's powerful, and it's here for you.*** It represents a genuine paradigm shift, moving software creation from the exclusive domain of traditional programmers towards a more accessible, conversational, and intuitive process. You, the artist, the writer, the entrepreneur, the educator, the expert in *your* field, now have an unprecedented opportunity to directly participate in building the digital tools and experiences you envision, using the power of your ideas and your words.

Throughout this book, we've aimed to demystify the process. We met the AI co-creators ready to assist you, walked step-by-step through building a project using conversational prompts, learned the crucial art of communicating your intent effectively, explored the kinds of amazing things you can build, and discussed how to navigate this new territory safely and responsibly.

As you step forward from here, remember the essential balance. **Embrace the incredible ease, speed, and creative potential** that Vibe Coding offers. Let it accelerate your prototyping, help you automate tasks, and empower you to bring simple applications to life in ways that were previously unimaginable without deep technical skills or significant investment. Let your intuition and your unique "vibe" guide the process.

But also, **always pair that excitement with mindful creation.** Remember the principles of Responsible Vibing we discussed. Test your creations thoroughly – not just the "happy path," but the edge cases too. Does it truly do what you expect? Start with simple, manageable projects to build your confidence and skills before tackling complexity. Be extremely cautious with sensitive data, always prioritizing security and leveraging trusted third-party services for things like payments and logins. Save your work often, creating safety nets against glitches or mistakes. Don't be afraid to seek a "second opinion," even from another AI. And crucially, engage your critical thinking – question the AI's output, use your common sense, and never trust blindly. Balancing the creative "vibe" with this practical awareness is key to a successful and sustainable journey.

Now, the most important part: **It's time for you to take action.** Reading about Vibe Coding is one thing; experiencing it is another entirely. The real learning, the real magic, happens when you start *doing*.

Don't wait for the "perfect" idea or until you feel like an "expert" prompter. Dive in!

- **Experiment with the tools:** Go back to Chapter 4, pick one of the accessible tools like ChatGPT, Claude, or Replit, sign up for a free account, and just start talking to it. Ask it simple questions, give it small tasks. Get a feel for the interaction.

- **Try the sample project:** Walk through the "Personal Movie Watchlist" project from Chapter 5 yourself, using your chosen tool. Experience the iterative loop of prompting, testing, and refining firsthand.
- **Start your own small idea:** What's a simple tool or webpage you've wished existed? A personal goal tracker? A landing page for a hobby project? A generator for creative writing prompts? Pick something small and try building the very first version using Vibe Coding. Don't aim for perfection; aim for progress.

Don't be afraid to stumble. The AI might misunderstand you. You might get unexpected results. You might hit a temporary roadblock. That's all part of the learning process! Treat it as an experiment, a conversation. Learn from each interaction, refine your prompts, and keep iterating. The barrier to entry is lower than ever before.

Most importantly, **never underestimate the value of your own creativity and ideas.** You possess unique insights, perspectives, and experiences that the world needs. Technology is ultimately just a tool; its true power lies in the human vision it helps bring to life. Vibe Coding is exciting precisely because it offers a new way to bridge the gap between your unique vision and tangible digital creation. Your ideas for apps, websites, tools, games, and interactive experiences are valuable. Your ability to communicate that vision is now your superpower.

The future of creation is becoming more accessible, more conversational, more *vibey*. It's a future you don't have to just watch unfold – you can actively participate in shaping it.

Your Next Steps:

Ready to jump in? Here are a few concrete actions you can take right now:

1. **Choose Your Tool:** Pick one of the beginner-friendly AI tools discussed in Chapter 4 (like ChatGPT, Claude, or Replit) and create a free account.
2. **Revisit the Walkthrough:** Try building the "Personal Movie Watchlist" from Chapter 5 yourself, following the steps and adapting the prompts as needed for your chosen tool.
3. **Brainstorm Simply:** Jot down 1-3 ideas for *very simple* tools or web pages that *you* would find useful or fun. Think MVP!
4. **Prompt Away:** Choose one simple idea and write your very first prompt for it. See what happens!
5. **Explore Communities:** Search online for communities of makers, AI creators, or users of the specific tool you chose. Reading about others' experiences can be inspiring and helpful.

The journey of a thousand miles begins with a single step. Your Vibe Coding journey begins with that first prompt.

Thank you for joining me through this exploration. I hope this book has served as a helpful and encouraging guide. The tools are ready, the potential is vast, and your ideas are waiting.

Go create. Find your vibe. Shape the future.

APPENDIX: RESOURCES FOR VIBING

This book aimed to give you a running start into the world of Vibe Coding. But the journey doesn't end here! The field of AI and creative tools is constantly evolving, and connecting with communities and further resources can be incredibly helpful. Here's a curated list to get you started:

1. AI Coding Assistants & Platforms (Your Co-Creators)

These are some of the key tools mentioned in the book, particularly suited for getting started without deep technical knowledge:

- **ChatGPT (OpenAI):** A powerful and widely accessible conversational AI excellent for generating code snippets, explaining concepts, debugging help, and brainstorming.
  - *Website:* https://chat.openai.com (or search for OpenAI ChatGPT)
- **Claude (Anthropic):** Another highly capable conversational AI known for its strong context understanding and thoughtful responses, also great for coding assistance and explanation.
  - *Website:* https://claude.ai (or search for Anthropic Claude)
- **Replit:** An online platform providing an integrated environment (code editor, file management, execution, AI tools) directly in your browser. Excellent for web projects and streamlining the code-test-refine loop. Often has specific AI features built-in.
  - *Website:* https://replit.com (or search for Replit)
- **(Other tools mentioned for context):**
  - *GitHub Copilot:* AI pair programmer integrated into code editors, primarily focused on code completion. (https://github.com/features/copilot)
  - *Cursor:* An AI-first code editor designed around chat and code generation features. (https://cursor.sh)

2. Learning Prompting (Communicating Effectively)

Mastering the "art of the prompt" (Chapter 6) is key. While specific guides change rapidly, here are places to look for beginner-friendly advice:

- **Official AI Tool Documentation/Blogs:** Check the websites of the tools you use (OpenAI, Anthropic, Replit, etc.). They often publish guides, tips, and examples for effective prompting.
- **Reputable Tech Blogs & Newsletters:** Many tech blogs (search for topics like AI, generative AI, prompt engineering for beginners) publish articles with practical prompting tips and techniques.
- **Online Course Platforms:** Sites like Coursera, Udemy, or edX may offer introductory courses on prompt engineering or using generative AI tools. Look for beginner-focused options.

- **General Search:** Try searching online for "prompt engineering tips for beginners," "how to write good ChatGPT prompts for coding," or similar phrases. Be critical and look for clear, practical advice.

3. Maker & AI Communities (Connect and Learn)

Learning alongside others can be incredibly valuable. Online communities provide places to ask questions, share your projects (even simple ones!), see what others are building, and get inspired.

- **Reddit:** Several subreddits are highly relevant:
  - r/ChatGPTCoding: Focused specifically on using ChatGPT for coding tasks.
  - r/artificialintelligence / r/AI: Broader discussions about AI, often including new tools and techniques.
  - r/programming / r/learnprogramming: While more technical, you can sometimes find discussions about AI's impact or beginner questions.
  - r/SideProject / r/IndieHackers: Communities focused on building projects, often featuring discussions about tools (including AI and no-code).
- **Maker Forums:** Search for general "maker forums," "indie developer communities," or forums specific to the type of project you're interested in (e.g., web development forums, game development forums).
- **Discord Servers:** Many communities related to AI tools, specific programming niches, or maker movements have active Discord servers for real-time chat and support.
- **Platform-Specific Communities:** Tools like Replit often have their own official forums or Discord servers where users can connect.

4. Further Reading & Context (Optional Deep Dives)

If you're interested in the origins and ongoing discussions around Vibe Coding:

- **Andrej Karpathy's Writings/Posts:** Search for his name along with "vibe coding" to find his original posts (likely on platforms like X/Twitter or blogs) from early 2025 that helped popularize the term.
- **Insightful Blog Posts:** Look for articles discussing the Vibe Coding phenomenon from different perspectives. Examples mentioned conceptually in the source document include:
  - Articles exploring large-scale code generation via AI (like Austin Starks' pieces).
  - Blog posts offering critical or skeptical takes on the practice (like the "makes me want to throw up" example, illustrating the strong opinions it generates).

- o Discussions on platforms like Medium (within tech-focused publications like CodeX) or individual developer blogs often cover emerging trends like Vibe Coding.

Remember, the best resource is often experimentation combined with community interaction. Don't hesitate to try things out, ask questions, and share your journey! Happy Vibing!

ABOUT THE AUTHOR

Akash Kumar Nayak combines a fascination for the mechanics behind our digital world with a Computer Science background from Indira Gandhi National Open University (IGNOU). As a tech enthusiast constantly exploring innovation, Akash became intrigued by the potential of AI-driven tools like those behind Vibe Coding to democratize digital creation. This book stems from that interest, aiming to bridge the gap between emerging technical capabilities and practical empowerment for aspiring creators. Akash's writing seeks to make cutting-edge concepts accessible, reflecting a belief in technology's power to unlock creative potential for everyone, regardless of their coding background.